WOMEN OF THE COURT

WOMEN
OF THE
COURT

INSIDE THE WNBA

Juliette Terzieff

alyson books
NEW YORK

Manufactured in the United States of America

Published by Alyson Books
245 West 17th Street, New York, NY 10011

Distribution in the United Kingdom
by Turnaround Publisher Services Ltd.
Unit 3, Olympia Trading Estate, Coburg Road, Wood Green
London N22 6TZ England

First Edition: May 2008

08 09 10 11 12 13 14 15 16 17 █ 10 9 8 7 6 5 4 3 2 1

ISBN: 1-59350-051-3
ISBN-13: 978-1-59350-051-1

Library of Congress Cataloging-in-Publication data are on file.

Cover design by Victor Mingovits
Interior design by Elliott Beard

For the women whose love of hoops has driven the game,
whose dedication empowers all women.

And my parents, George and Vaerie Terzieff,
who always believed that the measure of one's greatness
lies in one's intent and actions, not one's bank account.

Contents

CONTENTS

Foreword

By Betty "B-Money" Lennox

The game of basketball means a lot more to me than just a ball and a hoop to shoot for—it represents a chance to express myself and live out my dreams.

Growing up on a small farm in Oklahoma there was always plenty of hard physical work for me to do—animals to be fed, crops to be picked, bales of hay to be tossed. Hard days' labor under the sun or in rain or any kind of weather put food on the evening table. My family and I worked together as a team, shouldering the responsibility of building lives. I didn't do it for myself; I did it for the family. We all did.

But basketball? Basketball was, and still is, my passion, my escape, my place to be me.

The sense of freedom the game gives me allows me to express my emotions . When I'm on the court I'm happy. When this world tries to get me down, I have a place to work through it, give expression to my feelings, and recover my balance.

When I started playing the game my brothers were my opponents. It wasn't easy, as they were tough on me. But my mother told me I could not cry if I wanted to play with them. It took time, and a lot of hard work, but

I learned to beat them. I got tough. I knew I could achieve anything if I put my mind to it, with determination and faith. . . and I knew I wanted to keep playing basketball.

Basketball, and the quest to play, has taught me life lessons that have helped me become a better person. Hard work, dedication, discipline, the overcoming of odds, working with others to achieve a common goal—basketball has given me all these gifts of wisdom over the years. I've taken these lessons and used them both on, and off, the court.

But perhaps most important, the journey for me from small town to the highest levels of women's basketball has reinforced the life lesson that you should do what you love. When I go to work, I love it, and the hard work associated with my job is a joy, not a labor. Be the best at whatever you choose to do, and enjoy each step of the way. Take time out to really think about what it is you want to do and not what others want you to. I have an equation that I follow in my own life: FAITH+EDUCATION+ DETERMINATION = SUCCESS. Believe in yourself, then educate yourself on what it is you want to do and go to school and graduate. Set goals and go after them, because you can only be successful if you try. PLAY IT, LIVE IT, LOVE IT.

There is no time like the present to be a female basketball player in the United States. The women of generations past have paved the way for some remarkable players and a league that would not have been possible a few decades ago. I hope that today's athletes can continue to inspire the young ladies coming forward.

It feels good to be a part of something that people around the world look up to and respect. In other countries fans treat us like the followers of NBA stars in the States. Hopefully, the female players of today can keep it going to inspire future generations of young ladies so they can have the experience of showing their talent in an arena, with their families watching with pride.

I want young girls who read this book to be inspired to achieve any goal they want in life. It doesn't have to be about basketball or sports. You need to feel a sense of pride and invest time and energy toward your future, make plans on how you want your life to be, and don't let anyone stand in your way. And if it happens to be basketball or sports that you've chosen, be prepared for certain challenges. Do not let yourself get pushed down; you will get pushed but the key is: *How will you react?* Love what it is you want to do and do what it takes to fulfill your dream. Never stop dreaming.

February 10, 2008

Introduction

Writing this book ended up being as much of a learning experience for this author as I hope it will be for any new fan to the WNBA who picks it up to read. The contributions and steadfast efforts of the women chronicled in these pages are a testament to much more than just the pursuit of a worthy game.

As a journalist specializing in conflict situations and human rights, I have spent my days, nights, weekends immersed at times in much of the uglier side of humanity—chronicling the best and worst humanity has to offer in far-flung, conflict-ridden places, including Kosovo, Serbia, Pakistan, Afghanistan, Syria, and Turkey. Most of my work has centered around politics, economics, and human rights, even after my return to the United States in late 2004. Every day I have spent hours trolling through the world's media with CNN or BBC America on the television set in my office—wincing often as the bad news pours in; rejoicing on those rare occurrences that something truly uplifting finds its way onto the international news radar. The quest to find inspiring stories in the midst of great tragedy has been the soul of my journalistic career; and the hope these stories inspire is what has kept me in the game through some very dark times.

I thought that writing a book on women's basketball would take me down a more light-hearted road, along which I could examine the contributions of women to what might not routinely be considered a "mainstream" career undertaking for American females. How naïve I was. What I discovered is that women basketball players have faced down the challenges thrown at them by American society—stood in the face of derision, fought to overcome discrimination, hooped their way past the smirks of the many along the way who laughed at their efforts. Like American women in general, female basketball players have worked extremely hard to carve out an accepted place for themselves where they are comfortable in the tapestry of American culture. These women have created a legacy for the generations to come and I hope I have done their efforts justice.

After being immersed in research, attending games, and talking to those in and around the basketball world, I would still not characterize myself as a women's basketball "expert," able to quote jersey numbers, scoring percentages, or individual player histories at the drop of a hat. I am, however, a WNBA fan—thankful to the women (and men!) who helped me take this journey, and eager to accompany them from the stands as they continue to play the game.

January 23, 2008
Tampa, Florida

ONE

Why the WNBA?

Women's basketball boasts a long and demonstrably determined history built upon the efforts of tens of thousands of dedicated women, who played a game they loved hoping one day the United States would have a professional league of its own. Along the way players battled gender bias, racial discrimination, and societal dictates—always operating outside the mainstream; always challenged, rarely rewarded. Even now, well in to the twenty-first century, the women of basketball and their supporters face continuous challenges to keep the dream alive. As women's hoops history illustrates (as discussed in later chapters) changes in American society, culture, and perceptions have helped women ballers push the dream forward—but not to a point where a league like the WNBA is a guarantee.

Despite growing legions of female fans and players, the undeniable success of university-level women's basketball, and the deep pockets of a big brother sponsor in the form of the National Basketball Association, the WNBA still remains an entity that has yet to garner the public or financial support that would guarantee it the success female ballers rightly deserve for their efforts.

So why take on what—from certain perspectives—can best be described as a calculated risk? For some the answer is a matter of future business possibilities; for others a matter of doing the right thing to recognize the development of the game and the future it holds for generations of American women to come.

Across the sports world, owners are finding that the number of female fans is on the increase. More women are playing sports, more women are watching sports, and more women are spending money on sports-related merchandise. While the idealists see a world of opportunity for women's sports, the business-minded see millions of potential customers for their products.

Passage of Title IX of the Education Amendments of 1972, which outlawed sex discrimination in any educational program receiving federal funds, opened the floodgates for girls' sports, mandating educational institutions implement female programs to match their existing men's sports programs. Implementation in the ensuing years led to increases in female athletic participation of 904 percent at the high school level and 456 percent at the collegiate level as of 2007, according to the East Meadow, New York–based Women's Sports Foundation. These increases represent millions of young women, over three million in 2007 alone, with an inclination for sports. Interest in playing sports, especially among men, often translates into interest in watching sports and emulating one's sports heroes. While women appear less inclined to the transfer of interest, the female market still represents millions, if not billions, of potential sales dollars.

Most major sports now count females as over one-third of their fan base, and marketing over the last several years has increasingly shifted to reflect that reality as the number of female fans rises. The NBA, National Football League, National Hockey League, NASCAR, and Major League Baseball all offer fashion merchandise targeted directly at women—opening up partnership and sponsorship deals for the sports with a wider array of companies than ever before, including the likes of Harlequin Enterprises Ltd., the publisher of Harlequin romance novels* For the NBA alone, women's products resulted in over $100 million in sales in 2005. The NBA's 2007–2008 line of products for women featured jerseys, shirts, jackets, watches, headbands, jewelry, and slippers. Football's NFL for Her and the NHL's merchandise lines also include a range of team-centered clothing, purses, watches, and jewelry.

The growth of female fandom couldn't have come at a better time for sports leagues. Official merchandise sales is a multibillion dollar a year business that saw growth in the early 1990s take it above the $13 billion mark before dropping back down to around $10 billion by 2001.[†] By 2006, the sales figure was back up above $13 billion, a benchmark figure it again surpassed in 2007.[‡] While the increase may not be solely attributed to women, the steadily increasing popularity among females—who make up just over 50 percent of the American population and control billions of dollars in consumer spending capability—is a definite selling point for owners, leagues, merchandisers, and retailers.

Looking at sports marketing from a bigger-picture point of view, the NBA's decision to help fund and build the WNBA (see chapter 2 for more) was based in the belief that the WNBA will not only capitalize on young girls looking for female role models they can emulate, but also provide another vehicle to induct more women and families into the ranks of the NBA fan base, thus increasing ticket purchases, merchandise sales revenues, and other components that earn profit for the league. It's a strategy for which some measurable argument can be made—viewer numbers for NBA games have been climbing pretty steadily since the mid-1990s—especially among women—a benefit some see as a result, in part, of the publicity and support

---

*"Sports Teams Find a Lucrative Market in Women Enthusiasts"; *Southeast Missourian,* September 17, 2006.
[†]"NFL Merchandisers Catch On, Run with Women's Products"; *USA Today,* January 5, 2005.
[‡]The Licensing Letter; EPM Communications, Inc., January 7, 2008.

among women for the WNBA. The categorization of the WNBA as a prized ambassador for the sport of basketball is part of what has kept the NBA committed to supporting the league through its developmental—read: nonprofit making—first decade. Most of the WNBA teams continue to lose money, necessitating that the NBA provide annual financial help to the tune of $12 million to the WNBA as the league crossed the decade mark.*

"We have a good strategic reason to support the WNBA, which is the growth of viewership and fans for basketball. Our mission is to promote and grow the sport of basketball. The WNBA is precisely within the strategic bull's-eye of whatever we do," NBA Commissioner David Stern told the *Washington Post* in July 2006 of the league's commitment to its sister organization.

While it might not be considered terribly politically correct to say so, many within the basketball community at large view the WNBA as something the women deserve even if the league will never command the kind of following it needs to be truly competitive profitwise with the male leagues. For over one hundred years women who love the game have battled their way through whatever roadblocks society placed before them to not only keep the women's game alive, but watch it thrive. Amateur level women's basketball—whether it be the national teams playing in the Olympics and other international tournaments or American university teams winning their way to NCAA Championships—has a massive following in American society. Of course, for every one who will readily admit support for the idea that women ballers deserve a shot at helping make the WNBA work as a reward for decades of toil, there are two others who will deride it as liberal, feel-good mumbo jumbo.

Yet there are quite a few deep pockets that believe the WNBA will prove the naysayers wrong and emerge, at some point farther into its second decade of play, as a league able to stand financially on its own with a cadre of partners and sponsors. Already players, teams, and leagues have inked

---

*"A Matter of Value Instead of Profit"; *Washington Post,* July 12, 2006.

deals with Nike, Ocean Spray, Microsoft, Starbucks, T-Mobile, Toyota, and other big-name companies. With games broadcast in 203 countries in over 30 languages in 2007, and a new multiyear deal with ABC/ESPN to carry it through the year 2016, the NBA isn't the only business to believe in the potential of the WNBA. And at the end of the day, perhaps a women's professional league doesn't have to compete directly on a financial basis with existing men's leagues, but rather lay the groundwork, and standard, for future women's professional leagues in other sports.

Any honest assessment of what makes the WNBA a worthwhile endeavor must also include an homage to the feel-good atmosphere the WNBA players create around their teams, the league, and the sport. WNBA players may not routinely make headlines in the sports news the way their male counterparts do, but they occupy a valuable niche among young boys and girls through their individual accessibility and high-profile efforts within the communities where they play, work, and live (see chapters 8 and 11 for more details). Their devotion to the sport, and to promoting the sport amongst youngsters, is perhaps a natural extension of their campaign to carve out a place in the male-dominated sports world, but it also gives the league and its players a valuable emotional link to the fans. For American women, who, in general, tend to view athletes above and beyond their actions in the game and like to include their "lives" in the athletic hero story, this emotional bond is a powerful selling point. That the players are overwhelmingly friendly, engaging, well spoken, educated, and . . . oh . . . yes, talented, adds to the positive reaffirmation many seek in their sports heroes.

On the court the women play a different game than the men, with less emphasis on individual skills showcasing and more emphasis on teamwork. While competitive, the games are predominantly friendly matchups (at least until the playoff and championship season raises emotional on-court temperatures). While some basketball fans find this tedious and less exciting than the men's game—and seek to needle WNBA fans over the perceived lack of technical prowess for big plays amongst the female players—plenty of basketball purists admire the women's more down-to-earth playing styles.

The question whether the WNBA will prove to be as successful as leagues like the NBA is unlikely to be answered for several decades. And while plenty of people like to compare the two's prospects and argue that the WNBA—based on numbers (revenue, fan presence in arenas, etc.)—should not exist, these arguments ignore the very real facets of American society that demand a professional league for women as well as the fact that comparing long-established men's leagues (which themselves once struggled to get out of the red) to relatively young and untested women's leagues is an unfair comparison that places an unreasonable burden on the league. The WNBA fills a niche need within American society, one that has been ignored for a long time and that has finally—with the birth and many successes of the young league—found a way to capitalize on the hopes and hard work of tens of thousands of women who have devoted their lives to the game they love.

TWO

How the WNBA Came to Be

To say that the WNBA began on April 24, 1996, when the National Basketball Association Board of Governors approved the WNBA concept, would certainly be considered as accurate—but the truth is that the league did not spring into being at the snap of the NBA's fingers. The idea of a women's professional basketball league had been around well over a decade, and had been tried in a few different permutations with varying levels of success; none of them successful enough to last more than a few years before folding. The creation of the WNBA was built on the efforts of those who had come before—hoping to fulfill the promise so many hoped existed for the women's game.

With the expansions in American collegiate women's basketball programs as part of the post-Title IX women's sports boom, and an increasing international profile of the game throughout the 1970s and 1980s, the most natural next step was the creation of a women's professional league. Women's basketball, as of 1976, became an Olympic sport and professional leagues began to proliferate across Europe and Asia.

The first serious American contender came into being as the brainchild of Bill Byrne, who hoped to cash in on the appeal of the 1976 Olympics and upcoming publicity for the 1980 Games and spearheaded efforts to set up the Women's Professional Basketball League (WBL). Eight teams were named and funded to the tune of fifty thousand dollars, and the league prepared to launch its 1978 season.

After a fairly successful first season the WBL saw one team fold, but seven expansion teams joined the league ahead of its second season. "Machine Gun Molly" Bolin Kazmer and Ann Meyers emerged as the league's stars. Yet even with the star power and solid play, by the end of the second season two more teams had folded and financial difficulties, including late paychecks, curtailed travel expenses, and rising debt, began to take a toll. League owners ousted founder Bill Byrne, setting the tone for a troubled third—and what would ultimately be the WBL's final—season.

The WBL began its 1980–1981 season by losing four of the remaining teams (including the championship teams from the first two seasons, Houston and New York). The United States boycotted the 1980 Olympics, destroying any chance of rollover publicity, and the financial problems mounted. By the time the season ended two more teams had folded and league ownership decided to call it quits.

Others tried to organize what they hoped would be the first enduring American women's professional league in the 1980s and early 1990s but found little success. A WBL rival league, the Ladies Professional Basketball Association, formed during the 1980–1981 season hoping to benefit from the WBL's financial woes, but poor organization led the league to fold after only five games. In 1991, the Liberty Basketball Association thought gimmicks such as a nine feet, two inches high basket and skintight leotards might be the secret recipe for success, but played only one exhibition game appearance before folding.

It wasn't until the middle of the 1990s that truly realistic hopes for a lasting league really began to rise. The American Basketball League was founded in 1995 and began play in 1996, hoping to capitalize on a surge in women's basketball popularity following the U.S. women's team's undefeated gold medal run at the 1996 Olympics, growing female interest in watching sports, and the continuing rise of female participation in sports at the high school and collegiate levels. Eight teams played during the inaugural season, a number which jumped to nine in the second season. The league was popular with players and attracted future WNBA standouts like Katie Smith, Yolanda Griffith, Jennifer Azzi, and Sheri Sam, as it provided stock options, a retirement plan, and a seat at the board of governors table.

At the same time, the NBA was moving forward with plans to form the WNBA, and the ABL would ultimately find itself unable to compete financially. Even though attendance figures were steadily rising, the only place the ABL was able to secure television coverage was on regional networks and BET. Even with the WNBA lockout in the third season, the ABL was unable to secure the support or exposure it needed.

Citing a complete lack of operating funds, and no viable sponsorship or television opportunities on the horizon, the ABL Board of Governors filed for Chapter 11 bankruptcy protection in December 1998, in the middle of the league's third season, leaving a clear field for the NBA-funded WNBA to make its mark.

From the time the NBA approved the WNBA concept there was a feeling that this league, above all the others before it, had the best chance at success. The NBA had several decades of experience running an immensely popular league and plenty of money available to outlast any growing pains their new women's league might experience.

From the outset, the WNBA sought to stock its teams with the biggest women's basketball star power available, holding a four-part draft ahead of the 1997 season for its initial eight teams. The eight—Charlotte, Cleveland, Houston, Los Angeles, New York, Phoenix, Sacramento, and Utah—were each assigned two players in January 1997 in the first phase. Players such as Cynthia Cooper, Rebecca Lobo, Michelle Timms, and Sheryl Swoopes were among the presigned players. A month later the league held an Elite Draft for players who were no longer in college, bringing in more women's basketball pros, including Janeth Arcain, Kym Hampton, Nancy Lieberman, and Lynette Woodard. In April the WNBA held a more traditional draft for college-level players ahead of a fourth-stage final roster allocation period.

On June 21, 1997, the WNBA played its first game, a classic East Coast–West Coast smack down between the Los Angeles Sparks and the New York Liberty in L.A.'s Great Western Forum. Sparks guard Penny Toler would

IN THEIR OWN WORDS

KYM HAMPTON

Hampton not only played in the WNBA's inaugural game between the New York Liberty and Los Angeles Sparks, she started it, literally—matched up against Lisa Leslie on the opening tip-off—before going on to become one of the WNBA's first and most enduring legends. Hampton had played several years in Europe and Asia before the WNBA's 1997 Elite Draft brought her back across the ocean to play on home court. Hampton cherishes the memories of playing in the States and of retiring at Madison Square Garden in 2000 in front of 15,000 of her greatest fans.

I still get goose bumps as I remember sitting on the bus that took me and my Liberty teammates down in the tunnel of the Great Western Forum for that very first game. It felt like we had finally arrived, we finally did it. I always believed a pro league would happen in the States; I just wasn't sure I'd be around to play in it. I just felt so incredibly blessed.

As we got off the bus there must have been a hundred cameras, all with glaring lights staring in our faces. It was as if each one was trying to get something from one of our blank faces that would give them a lead on how the game would go. Those faces were masking a rollercoaster of emotions. When we got to the locker room, I sat in my locker space and wondered how many great legends had sat in this same space. I thought about all the women before us—the Ann Meyers, the Carol Blazejowskis—and the

score the WNBA's first basket, but the visiting Liberty would become the first WNBA team to win a competitive game, beating the Sparks 67–57. By the time the Houston Comets would lift the WNBA Championship trophy less than three months later on August 30, 1996, everyone associated with the league was confident the WNBA was on the right track.

In its first season, the WNBA posted average game attendance of 9,669

Photo Credit: Courtesy of Kym Hampton

perseverance to keep playing no matter what people said. They paved the way, and that night I was overwhelmed.

We were dressed and ready for the game when we arrived so we went out to the court to get some shots in. Each time I shot I couldn't help but think that in an hour and a half the whole world would be watching us. I was so excited to think friends and family would get to see me play, and in the league's first game, matched up against Lisa

WNBA legend Kym Hampton

Leslie on that tip-off—all of it, it was more that I ever would have dared to hope for.

Adapted from conversations with Kym Hampton and her written commentary on Off-Court.com

spectators—almost three times the amount of the ABL—proving to be an immediate hit with women's basketball fans.

Over the next eleven years, the fans' love for the league would intensify even as in-arena attendance figures slumped, leading some teams to fold and be replaced in other cities. The NBA would take annual financial losses

WNBA TIMELINE
HIGHLIGHTS IN THE WNBA'S HISTORY

April 24, 1996   NBA Board of Governors approves WNBA concept

October 23, 1996   Sheryl Swoopes and Rebecca Lobo become first players to formally sign on to play in the new league

October 30, 1996   Eight locations selected to host WNBA charter teams are Charlotte, Cleveland, Houston, Los Angeles, New York City, Phoenix, Sacramento, and Utah

February 27, 1997   WNBA holds Elite Draft for sixteen signed veteran players; Dana Head is selected first

April 19-22, 1997   WNBA holds first-ever predraft camp in Orlando with over four dozen participants

April 28, 1997   First draft for college players and unsigned veterans; Tina Thompson selected first

June 21, 1997   Inaugural season opens with the New York Liberty beating the Los Angeles Sparks, 67–57

August 30, 1997   Houston Comets win first-ever WNBA Championship

October 1, 1997   WNBA announces expansion teams in Detroit and Washington will join league beginning in the 1998 season

April 22, 1998   WNBA announces expansion teams in Orlando and Minnesota will join the league beginning in the 1999 season

on the league and the WNBA would struggle to find its marketing footing, but the passion behind the league would leave no room for talk of abandoning the undertaking. Even now the WNBA continues to experience growing pains, but the league, most players and fans believe, is here to stay. Corporate sponsors continue to demonstrate financial support for individual players,

June 7, 1999 WNBA announces expansion teams in Indiana, Miami, Portland, and Seattle will join the league beginning in the 2000 season

July 14, 1999 WNBA plays its first All-Star game

July 27, 1999 Houston Comets's Sheryl Swoopes first to record a triple-double in the WNBA, with fifteen points, fourteen rebounds, and ten assists in Houston win over the Detroit Shock

August 1, 2001 Los Angeles Sparks become first WNBA team to go undefeated for a season at home

July 30, 2002 Los Angeles Sparks's Lisa Leslie becomes first woman in WNBA to dunk in a game with a one-handed layup

September 14, 2003 Seattle Storm's Lauren Jackson becomes first international player to be named WNBA's Most Valuable Player

August 18, 2005 Anne Donovan becomes first WNBA female coach to win one hundred games

June 25, 2006 Los Angeles Sparks's Lisa Leslie becomes the first player to score five thousand points in the WNBA

teams, and the league. While the deals may not be on par with the billion-dollar agreements in the NBA or other men's leagues, the business world's ongoing commitment to the WNBA is just one of the many reasons to have high hopes for the league.

With a constant influx of young talent from the collegiate ranks and a brand new ESPN television deal announced in July 2007 that will take the league through it second decade, women's basketball fans have plenty to cheer about.

THREE

Hoops History

No look at the history of the United States's first enduring women's professional basketball league could possibly be considered complete without looking farther back at the tens of thousands of women and girls who have played the game since Senda Berenson Abbott adapted the rules of Dr. James Naismith's newly invented game of basketball for women's play in 1892.

Within four years after Berenson Abbott, known as the Mother of Women's Basketball, recalibrated the game to reflect a more feminine approach, women's basketball saw its first intercollegiate game, between Stanford University and the University of California at Berkeley in 1896. Thus began a tradition that would not only endure, but see the women's game grow to be one of amateur athletics's most popular sports.

In the century between that first intercollegiate matchup and the decision to move forward with the WNBA, an entire book's worth of history unfolded. What follows are highlights of some of the ups and downs women's basketball has faced along the way, and some of the women who helped get the game where it is today.

Berenson Abbott's original rules for the women's game seem quite quaint by modern standards—no snatching the ball, no more than a three-bounce dribble, and no running—but at a time when women were still in corsets, unable to vote, and subject to numerous societal limitations on public activity, the game was considered quite a progressive undertaking for women. Berenson's more feminine version of the game quickly demonstrated a widespread appeal to women and within three years was being played on campuses across the United States The popularity did not come without de-

HIGHLIGHTS FROM THE HISTORY OF WOMEN'S BASKETBALL

1892   Senda Berenson Abbott adapts rules of basketball for women's play

1896   America's first intercollegiate women's basketball game between Stanford University and the University of California at Berkeley

1899   First Women's Basketball Rules Committee forms with representatives of four women's schools in an attempt to standardize rules

1903   Rules committee shortens halves from twenty minutes to fifteen minutes

1910   Official rules change to outlaw dribbling

1913   Official rules change to allow return of the single dribble

1916   No coaching allowed during the game. No substitutions. No time-outs.

1918   Official rules change to allow use of substitutions

1926   Amateur Athletic Union sponsors first national women's basketball tournament

1934   Tulsa Business College wins first of three straight AAU titles

1936   All-American Red Heads formed

1953   First World Championships held; United States wins gold

tractors, both male and female, who worried the game was too strenuous and too unladylike for young girls.

In the earliest days of the twentieth century the game witnessed several rounds of rule changes and reformulations as it continued to win over fans and supporters. Dribbling, for example, underwent several changes from its original three-bounce limit, to being outlawed in 1910, to a single dribble returning in 1913 (continuous, unlimited dribble would not become the standard until 1966).The number of players on a team, types of legal passes,

1955 First Pan American Games basketball competition; United States wins gold

1962 Nashville Business College wins first of eight straight AAU titles

1966 Official rules changed to allow unlimited continuous dribbling

1971 Official rules change to set a five-player, full-court game with a thirty-second shot clock as the standard

1975 First Kodak All-American team named

1976 Women's basketball debuts at the Olympic Games

1978 Women's Professional Basketball League forms with eight teams

1978 Carol Blazejowski named inaugural recipient of the Wade Trophy

1982 First NCAA National Championship held

1984 U.S. women's team wins first Olympic gold

1986 Nancy Lieberman joins the USBL's Springfield Fame, becoming the first woman to play in a men's professional league

1996 American Basketball league forms

1997 WNBA launches

and length of play all also underwent changes during that period.

In 1926, the Amateur Athletic Union (AAU)—a nonprofit, volunteer sports organization around since 1888—reversed its earlier position against endorsing any public display of women's basketball and began sponsoring a national amateur women's basketball championship using men's rules to play the game. Over the next five decades (until after the 1972 passage of Title IX) AAU tournaments were the only title-bearing option for young women who wanted to play basketball after school. Teams from across the country—sponsored by businesses and educational institutions, including Frigidaire, Sunoco, Hanes, and the Tulsa Business College—played in the AAU tournaments, which continue today though with much less fanfare and a smaller following. In the roaring twenties the AAU tournament was still considered contentious by many, raising the ire of prominent society females and sports educators who decried the sight of young women in short shorts screaming at opponents even as fans turned out by the thousands to watch the teams battle it out. Whatever the controversy, the proliferation of women's teams in industrial cities across the United States was seen by business owners as good public relations.

Most of the women who played basketball in the first half of the twentieth century barely even register as footnotes in standard basketball knowledge today, but the tens of thousands of young American women who played in the AAU tournaments throughout the years out of love for the game helped keep the basketball dream alive for generations to come, at a time when there was no collegiate or professional level league (for women *or* men), and laid the groundwork for the advancement of women's sport in the latter part of the century. Only those truly well versed in women's basketball history may now know names like Carrie McElroy, Kate Carragher, Gypsy Williams, Grace Stuckey, and Laura McElreath. The five—collectively the Sun Oilers—would lose only two out of 554 games played between 1923–1930 and bring home three AAU titles to ecstatic Dallas fans. Similarly, Babe Didrikson of the Dallas Cyclones, long considered one of the twentieth century's finest female athletes, was once a household name. Didrikson was recruited straight out of her junior year in high school by the owner of the Employee Casualty Company (which owned the Cyclones), took the Cyclones to three straight AAU titles, and was named an AAU All-American.

If the AAU participating teams were the business model of women's basketball throughout the bulk of the twentieth century, the entertainment-savvy, barn-hopping teams from Middle America were the grass roots' heartfelt answer. They were women's basketball champions that never played for titles, but always played for fun—and won, against the men. Tough competitors with a flair for the kind of dramatics and tricks that would later catapult the Harlem Globetrotters to international fame, the All-American Red Heads were the best known of the professional teams of the time. The Red Heads were so popular that their travels across the country, which began in 1936, would continue up through the 1980s.

The team came into being, so the legend goes, on a lark when a local Cassville, Missouri, team made up of employees at a beauty salon owned by Doyle Olson, decided to dye their hair one night to match two of their red-headed teammates (twins Jo and Genevra Langerman) and played against a local men's team. The team was an immediate local hit and Doyle's husband C. M.—who ran his own men's traveling basketball team—saw an opportunity to take the Red Heads to a national audience. Beside skill with a basketball and a penchant for theatrics, Red Head hopefuls needed to have red hair, or be willing to dye it red. Even though women were still playing a six-on-six, half-court-adapted game, the Red Heads played the men by the men's rules—continuous dribble, full-court basketball.

The team proved so popular that later decades would see as many as three Red Head squads traveling the country at the same time. They were women's basketball's first true star professional team, even if they had to resort to tricks and gimmicks to make the game palatable for still-wary critics of the game. The women played about two hundred games in a seven-month season as they traveled tens of thousands of miles, and over the years compiled a

50 percent victory record in the games they played against men. When Olson sold the team to Orwell Moore in 1948, the Red Heads gained a prolific scorer in his wife, Lorene "Butch" Moore, who would go on to score over thirty-five thousand points in eleven seasons. AAU All-Americans Peggy Lawson and Hazel Walker also lent their talent to the Red Heads, with Walker later going on to form her own traveling team, the Arkansas Travelers.

Like the Red Heads, Hazel Walker's Arkansas Travelers moved around the country by station wagon, playing against men using men's rules as often as six nights a week. Some of her fellow Red Heads, including Allegra "Stubby" Winter and Mary Alice "Peaches" Hatcher, joined the Travelers. Winter, a towering five-foot two, was one of the early players to demonstrate that size is no match for heart, was one of the team's top scorers, and would delight fans with her signature "piggyback play"—where she would literally ride piggyback on a teammate's back to score a basket (a play she originally used as a Red Head). Walker, herself a prolific free thrower, would challenge all comers from the audience to free throw competitions during game half-times (and, of course, she usually won). The travelers played for sixteen seasons between 1949 and 1965, winning 85 percent of their games.

Like the women who played amateur basketball in the AAU, the thousands of women who played on the era's biggest barn-hopping teams did so for a love of the game, but with one major distinction: they got paid. These women were women's basketball's first professional players even if they weren't widely recognized as so in society. Didrikson, for example, was paid $75 a month to work as a secretary at the Employee Casualty Company, but she wasn't hired for her typing skills. Later in her career, Didrikson would command as much as $1,000 a month with her traveling coed team—a fortune in Depression-era America.

Though the game displayed sustainable popularity decade after decade, sports in general was still largely considered a pursuit ill-suited to young women, and women's basketball wouldn't begin to see real change—and real acceptance—until the 1970s.

Women's sports in America took a huge leap forward following the en-actment of Title IX of the Educational Amendments of 1972, which man-dated any education or athletic program receiving federal funding be open equally to males and females, leading to a massive proliferation of collegiate-level programs. As women's basketball programs expanded and improved at schools across the country, the National Collegiate Athletic Association (NCAA)—a century-old voluntary organization made up of American uni-versities and colleges to govern collegiate sporting programs—decided to take the next logical step and held the first NCAA Division 1 Women's Bas-ketball Championships tournament, which Louisiana Tech won, in 1982. Twenty-five years later the women's NCAA basketball tournament remains one of American amateur athletics's premier events.

There has been, and continues to be, plenty of politics and some acrimony surrounding Title IX and how enforcement of its provisions has affected men's sports programs, undoubtedly more than enough material to fill a chapter or two on its own. But by and large most people within the sporting world agree that Title IX has helped women's sports capitalize on building societal changes in the way we view athletic participation. Certainly wom-en's basketball is a prime example as the NCAA experience demonstrates.

"It's a logical connection, if not a legal one, to argue that the WNBA came about as a result of Title IX, but in reality there's nothing in Title IX that says you have to have a league," argues basketball fanatic and widely respected hoops writer Helen Wheelock. "At the same time, Title IX provided a plat-form from which to launch a professional league as a direct extension of more people watching college play."

In fact, Title IX was one element of a rapidly changing political and social landscape during the 1960s and 1970s that would also see women's basket-ball finally included as a competitive event on the world's largest sporting stage, in the 1976 Olympic Games. Only six teams competed that year—the Soviet Union, Japan, Bulgaria, Canada, the United States, and Czechoslo-vakia—and the U.S. women's team would put forth a silver medal-winning performance. Not oneAmerican athlete made it to the 1980 Moscow Games, as the United States led a multination boycott over the Soviet Union's 1979 invasion of Afghanistan. The women's team returned to the Olympics for the 1984 Los Angeles Games to win the gold medal—and have won every Olympic gold medal since then except for 1992.

The stage—or court—was set. The players had long been ready; societal conditions were appropriate . . . the time had come for the Women's National Basketball Association.

WOMEN'S BASKETBALL TRAILBLAZERS

Throughout basketball's one hundred-plus years of history, all the women who played the game have been beating a trail to society's acceptance of women in sports, and, for basketball, to the WNBA. Here are just a few of the remarkable women who have made immeasurable contributions to the game. While few of these women remain "household" names in modern American pop culture, the game of basketball would not be where it is today without their efforts.

Mildred "Babe" Didrikson-Zaharias (1911–1956)

Didrikson was an all-around athlete who excelled not only in basketball but in track and field, baseball, and golf.

Didrikson led the Employers Casualty team to a 1931 AAU championship title and headlined the short-lived Babe Didrikson's All-Americans, a coed traveling team that played one five-month season in 1934–1935.

Didrikson achieved Olympic glory during the 1932 Los Angeles Games, winning the first-ever women's javelin competition and the first-ever 80-meter hurdles, and brought home a silver in the high jump. As an amateur golfer, Didrikson won thirteen straight tournaments in 1946 and became the first American to win a British amateur title in 1947. Over the years, she racked up fifty-five tournament victories, including three U.S. Women's Opens, and in 1949 helped found the Ladies Professional Golf Association.

Didrikson was voted Associated Press Female Athlete of the Year six times and the Associated Press Greatest Female Athlete of the first half of the twentieth century in a 1950 poll.

Ora Mae Washington (1898-1971)

Washington is perhaps best remembered among the Philadelphia African American community as a prolific tennis champion who took home eight straight singles titles in the all-black American Tennis Association during twelve years of astonishingly superior play between 1924 and 1936. She also won every women's doubles championship between 1925 and 1936 with various partners, and won three mixed doubles titles in 1939, 1946, and 1947.

But for basketball fans Washington is remembered as the central force—as the center, leading scorer, and coach—of the Philadelphia Tribune's traveling team, the Hustle. Like the other traveling teams, the Hustle played against men and women, using men's rules and, during the 1930s, lost only six games. During her travels with the Hustle, Washington would often sponsor basketball clinics to teach other women and young girls about the game. Washington played basketball for eighteen years with various Philadelphia teams, but is best known for her time with the Hustle.

At the time black athletes were not allowed to profit from playing sports so Washington worked as a housekeeper to support herself. Washington would live out her days in relative obscurity in Philadelphia, occasionally returning to the colored YWCA in Germantown where she learned to play tennis to help coach young sports-minded girls. While she was considered one of the greatest athletes of the generation, segregation and discrimination prevented Washington from receiving recognition for her Herculean efforts.

Washington was posthumously inducted into the Black Athletes Hall of Fame in 1976.

Hazel Walker (1914-1990)

Walker spent fourteen years as an amateur player, earning seven AAU All-American selections, six national free throw titles, and four AAU titles during her time with the Tulsa Business College Stenos, Little Rock's Lewis, and Norwood Flyers. Walker was nominated Associated Press Female Athlete of the Year in 1940.

The Oak Hill, Arkansas, native subsequently spent three years with the All-American Red Heads before going on to form Hazel Walker's Arkansas Travelers. Walker played for thirty-seven years, nineteen of them as a professional, before retiring in 1965 at the age of fifty-one.

Walker was posthumously inducted into the Women's Basketball Hall of Fame in 2001.

Nera White (1935-)

This native of Macon County, Tennessee, played basketball with the Nashville Business College, taking them to ten AAU championship wins between 1955 and 1969. In the process, the six-foot-one center was named a record-setting, fifteen-time AAU All-American. White led the United States to a gold medal–winning performance at the 1957 World Championships in Rio de Janeiro, Brazil, and was named the series' Most Valuable Player. White also saw international action as a member of All-Star teams that toured Russia, Great Britain, Venezuela, Brazil, Germany, and France.

White was in the first pair of women to be inducted into the Naismith Memorial Basketball Hall of Fame in 1992, and was also inducted into the Women's Basketball Hall of Fame in 1999.

Lusia Harris-Stewart (1955-)

Harris-Stewart demonstrated her capabilities as a top caliber center during her years at Delta State University, where she scored 2,981 points, nabbed

1,662 rebounds, and graduated holding fifteen of the university's single game, team, and career records. During Harris-Stewart's tenure the team went 109–6 and won three straight Association for Intercollegiate Athletics for Women (AIAW) championships.

Harris-Stewart was the first woman ever drafted by an NBA team, when the New Orleans Jazz picked her in the 1977 draft. Harris-Stewart, who was pregnant at the time and figured the move was a bit of a publicity stunt for the Jazz, declined to attend training camp.

At the international level, Harris-Stewart helped the U.S. team take home a gold medal in the 1975 Pan American Games before moving on to play in the first-ever Olympic women's basketball competition in 1976. The United States won silver.

Harris-Stewart was inducted alongside Nera White into the Naismith Memorial Basketball Hall of Fame in 1992.

Lynette Woodard (1959–)

This Wichita, Kansas, native bounded onto the women's basketball scene as a four-time Kodak All-American at the University of Kansas, where she finished her collegiate career in 1981 with an all-time record-setting 3,649 points. Woodard is a two-time Olympian, though neither she nor the team would end up playing in 1980 as the United States boycotted the Moscow Games. Woodard would return in 1984 as cocaptain and help lead the U.S. team to a gold medal at the Los Angeles Games.

Woodard again made international headlines in 1985 when she became the first woman to sign on to play with the Harlem Globetrotters, with whom she would spend two years traveling the world and raising the profile of American female basketball players.

Woodard played professionally in Asia and Europe in the 1980s and early 1990s, helping her Sicily Priolo teammates bring home the Italian championship for the 1988–1889 season before retiring in 1993. In 1997, Woodard came out of retirement to play two seasons in the WNBA, first with the

Cleveland Rockers and then the Detroit Shock, achieving a lifelong dream of playing professional basketball in the United States.

Woodard was enshrined in the Naismith Memorial Basketball Hall of Fame in 2004 and the Women's Basketball Hall of Fame in 2005.

"Machine Gun Molly" Bolin Kazmer (1957–)

Bolin Kazmer was a standout player at her high school in Moravia, Iowa, and during her college years at Grandview College in Des Moines, but it was her tenacious play in the Women's Basketball League that put her in the record books. Bolin Kazmer was the first player signed by the league when she joined the Iowa Cornets, and in the WBL's second season she scored a record setting 32.8 points per game, giving her 1,179 points in a thirty-six-game season, and, shortly thereafter, the nickname "Machine Gun Molly."

While the league itself would only last three seasons, Bolin Kazmer was a tireless campaigner for the sport through her ferocious play on the court and her panache for public relations off it. She was the doomed league's poster girl and continued to run basketball clinics for girls and advocate for a professional women's basketball league long after the 1984 end of her professional career.

Nancy Lieberman (1958–)

Lieberman blasted onto the international scene before she'd even completed high school, as a member of the gold medal-winning 1975 World Championships women's team. At the ripe age of eighteen Lieberman became the youngest female basketball player on record to win an Olympic medal, a silver in the 1976 Games—also the first time women's basketball was included as an Olympic sport—a feat she followed with a silver medal-winning performance as part of the 1979 Pan American Games team.

Her collegiate career was equally stellar as the three-time Kodak All-American helped Old Dominion University win the 1979 and 1980 AIAW championships. Lieberman left school early to play professional basketball (but would return to Old Dominion in 2000 to complete her degree).

As a pro, Lieberman was the number-one draft choice in 1980 for the Women's Professional Basketball League's Dallas Diamonds. In 1986 Lieberman became the first female to play in a men's professional league with the Springfield Fame of the United States Basketball League, and then went on to play with the Washington Generals in 1987–1988 on their world tour with the Harlem Globetrotters. Lieberman played the inaugural WNBA season with the Phoenix Mercury before going on to coach the Detroit Shock for three years.

Lieberman was inducted into the Naismith Memorial Basketball Hall of Fame in 1996 and the Women's Basketball Hall of fame in 1999.

FOUR

The League: Western Conference

The WNBA's Western Conference has dominated championships—winning all but three in the last eleven years—and produced some of the league's most enduring stars. Like its counterpart in the East, the conference underwent some growing pains during the first decade as the Portland Fire survived only two seasons before folding and the Utah Starzz moved out of state in 2003 to San Antonio, Texas.

Each individual team maintains a Web site with extensive information not only about the team and its performance, but also information on special events and community outreach programs. Most of the team Web sites have dedicated fan sections, fan forums, and team-focused blog sections, which often contain blogs from active team members. Fans—new and old alike—can always find more detailed and often rabidly passionate information on the Internet provided by teams' fans (for suggestions of places to start, see chapter 12).

The following information is current as of the 2007 season.

*Western Conference 2007 All-Stars huddle with coach
Jenny Boucek during a Washington, D.C., practice session*

HOUSTON COMETS

Home Venue	Toyota Center, Houston, Texas
Mascot	HALEY, "The Houston Comets Far-Out Alien"
Team Colors	Red, white, blue
Owner	Hilton Koch
General Manager	Karleen Thompson
Coach	Karleen Thompson
Team Web site	www.wnba.com/comets/
Ticket Information	Available through team Web site or call 713-627-WNBA
For fans	The Comets Web site's fan-oriented sections include theme night information, video and picture galleries, and a link to where fans can get their hands on Comets gear.
Fan Mail	By E-mail: fanear@rocketball.com By Post: 1510 Polk Street Houston, TX 77002

More about the team: The Comets were one of the league's first eight teams when the WNBA launched in 1997. They flew out of the proverbial gates to take not only the first, but the second, third, and fourth WNBA championships under Coach Van Chancellor and his Triple Threat (Cynthia Cooper, Sheryl Swoopes, and Tina Thompson), becoming the WNBA's first official and, thus far, most enduring dynasty. Houston's glory was tempered with the 1999 loss of guard Kim Perrot to cancer. Perrot was awarded a third championship ring posthumously and was the first player to have her jersey retired.

LOS ANGELES SPARKS

Home Venue	Staples Center, Los Angeles, California
Mascot	SPARKY, a brown dog
Team Colors	Purple, gold, teal
Owner	Katherine E. Goodman and Carla Christofferson
General Manager	Penny Toler
Coach	Michael Cooper
Team Web site	www.wnba.com/sparks/
	www.myspace.com/losangelessparks
Tickets	Available through team Web site or call 877-44-SPARKS
For fans	The Sparks's Web site's fan-related material includes information on the teams' boosters (the SparKids and Ole Skool Crew), a link to the team's Hoopedia.com entry, and a community calendar.
Fan mail	888 S. Figueroa Street, Suite 2010
	Los Angeles, CA 90017

More about the team: The Sparks hosted the first-ever WNBA game against the New York Liberty on June 21, 1997, where then point guard and now General Manager Penny Toler scored the league's first points. Later, the Sparks looked to mount a challenge to the Houston Comet's dynasty with back-to-back WNBA Championship wins in 2001 and 2002 under Coach Michael Cooper, who left the Sparks after the 2004 season but returned in 2007. Led by veteran starting center Lisa Leslie, who missed the 2007 season to give birth to a daughter, the Sparks have remained a steady, strong contender in the Western Conference. Katherine Goodman and Carla Christofferson, a lawyer and a teacher respectively, took their die-hard fans' love and turned it into a purchase, buying the Sparks before the 2007 season.

MINNESOTA LYNX

Home Venue	Target Center, Minneapolis, Minnesota
Mascot	PROWL, a lynx
Team Colors	blue, green, white, silver
Owner	Glen Taylor
General Manager	Roger Griffith
Coach	Dan Zierden
Team Web site	www.wnba.com/lynx/
Tickets	Available through team Web site or call 612-673-8400
For fans	The Lynx Web site has an extensive fan section that includes downloadable wallpapers, e-cards, photo galleries, and promotion announcements.
Fan mail	By Post: Timberwolves/Lynx Offices
	600 First Avenue N
	Minneapolis, MN 55403

More about the team: The Lynx and the now-defunct Orlando Miracle joined the WNBA in the 1999 season as part of the WNBA's expansion efforts. Despite struggling through five coaches in the team's first eight years, the Lynx made back-to-back appearances in the WNBA Playoffs in 2003 and 2004. In May 2006, the Lynx set a league-best single game scoring record beating the Los Angeles Sparks 114–71, in an otherwise pretty dismal season where they ended up 10–24 despite the presence of Rookie of the Year Seimone Augustus. Even with the continued individual success of Augustus—who averaged 22.6 points per game—and the addition of number-one overall draft pick Lindsey Harding (who went down with a knee injury halfway through the season), 2007 ended up being hardly a better year for the team that ended the season at 10–24 again.

PHOENIX MERCURY

Home Venue	US Airways Center, Phoenix, Arizona
Mascot	Scorch, "a real hottie"
Team Colors	purple, red, chartreuse
Owner:	Jerry Colangelo
General Manager	Ann Meyers Drysdale
Coach	None (Paul Westhead resigned after 2007 Championship win)
Team Web site	www.wnba.com/mercury/
Tickets	Available through Web site or call 602-252-WNBA
For fans	The Mercury's Web site is packed with fan-friendly content, including screen savers, wallpaper, newsletter sign-ups, link to the team shop, and information on community events like the Mercury Fan Fest.
Fan mail	By e-mail: Form on Web site
	By post: 201 East Jefferson Street
	Phoenix, AZ 85004

More about the team: The Mercury was one of the WNBA's original eight teams and came out swinging with playoff appearances in 1997, 1998 (where they reached the Finals), and 2000, led by legendary basketball players Cheryl Miller, Michele Timms, Jennifer Gillom, and Nancy Lieberman. The team struggled to build on the early successes as its core players were traded or retired, but has reemerged in the last few years as contender with the additions of Diana Taurasi in 2004, and in 2006 Cappie Pondexter and Coach Paul Westhead, a former NBA coach who once coached the Los Angeles Lakers to a victorious 1980 NBA Final appearance. The Mercury stormed through the early rounds of the 2007 postseason on their way to challenge reigning champions the Detroit Shock at the WNBA Finals, where they emerged victorious after a grueling five-game series.

SACRAMENTO MONARCHS

Home Venue	ARCO Arena, Sacramento, California
Mascot	Monty, a gray dragon
Team Colors	purple, red, black, silver
Owner	Maloof Family, Maloof Sports & Entertainment
General Manager	John Whisenant
Coach	Jenny Boucek
Team Web site	www.wnba.com/monarchs/
Tickets:	Available through team Web site or call 916-928-3650
For fans	The Monarchs' Web site fan section includes video highlights, wallpaper downloads, a link to the official team store, a newsletter sign-up, and Monarchs fan photos.
Fan mail	By post: c/o ARCO Arena One Sports Parkway Sacramento, CA 95834

More about the team: The Monarchs launched in the WNBA's 1997 inaugural season and made their first playoff appearance in 1999. Over the next six years the Monarchs—led by the ubertalented pair of Ticha Penichiero and Yolanda Griffith—would make it back to the playoffs every year but one, finally emerging victorious over the Connecticut Sun at the 2005 WNBA Championship. After their win, the Monarchs became the first women's professional sports team to appear on a Wheaties cereal box.

SAN ANTONIO SILVER STARS

Home Venue	AT&T Center, San Antonio, Texas
Mascot	The Silver Fox
Team Colors	black, silver
Owner	Peter Holt
General Manager	Dan Hughes
Coach	Dan Hughes
Team Web site	www.wnba.com/silverstars
Tickets	Available through team Web site or call 210-444-5050
For fans	The Silver Stars Web site has one of the most extensive galleries of downloadable wallpaper of any of the WNBA teams. Fans can also find information on basketball camps for kids, how to sign up for the e-mail newsletter, and links to purchase Silver Stars gear.
Fan mail	One AT&T Center San Antonio, TX 78219

More about the team: The Silver Stars, one of the WNBA's first eight teams, was originally based in Salt Lake City, Utah, as the Starzz but moved to Texas in 2003 where the team became the San Antonio Silver Stars. The Starzz made playoff appearances in both 2001 and 2002, but the team struggled to find its footing after the move to San Antonio. Before the 2007 season, the Silver Stars acquired Becky Hammon and Ruth Riley to team up with returning players Vickie Johnson, Sophia Young, and Shanna Crossley, and raced out of the blocks in the early season to rack up the second best record in the league. San Antonio would make it to the Western Conference Championship series in 2007 where the team fell to the Phoenix Mercury.

SEATTLE STORM

Home Venue	Key Arena, Seattle, Washington
Mascot	Doppler, a maroon creature representing a weather system
Team Colors	dark green, red, gold
Owner	The Professional Basketball Club (Clay Bennett)
General Manager	Karen Bryant
Coach	Anne Donovan
Team Web site:	www.wnba.com/storm/
Tickets	Available through team Web site or call 206-217-WNBA
For Fans	The Storm Web site's fan content includes download-able wallpaper, sign-up information for the Seattle StormWatch newsletter, a large photo gallery, and a link to the Storm team shop.

More about the team: The Storm played its first season in 2000 and while the team got off to a rocky start the first couple of years, draft selections of soon-to-be WNBA stars Lauren Jackson in 2001 and Sue Bird a year later helped send the Storm to its first post-season appearance in 2002. Two years later the young Seattle team beat the Connecticut Sun to clinch the WNBA Championship. Along the way Australia native Jackson would become the first international player awarded the WNBA Most Valuable Player award in 2003—a feat she would repeat in 2007 after Phoenix defeated Seattle in the first round of the playoffs. After the July 2007 sale of the Storm and its NBA counterpart SuperSonics to the Oklahoma City–based Professional Basketball Club, serious doubts arose over whether the teams would remain beyond 2008 or be relocated.

FIVE

The League:
Eastern Conference

While the Western Conference reveled in its six straight WNBA Championships and early domination of the league, the Eastern Conference would have its own moments to celebrate in the inaugural decade. From the New York Liberty beating the Los Angeles Sparks on June 21, 1997, in the WNBA's first-ever game, to the Detroit Shock winning the Eastern Conference's first WNBA Championship in 2003, the conference proved its own penchant for glory could outshine the West. But the Eastern Conference also battled through some lows: losing two of the original franchises (the Cleveland Rockers after five seasons and the Charlotte Sting after ten); an aborted attempt to field a Miami team (the Sol) which lasted only two seasons; and a move up north for the Orlando Miracle to become the Connecticut Sun. In January 2007, the Charlotte Sting folded, leaving the Eastern Conference with only six teams to compete in the 2007 season against the Western Conference's seven teams.

As with the Western Conference, all of the Eastern Conference teams maintain Web sites with extensive information not only about the team, but also information on special events, community outreach efforts, and sections for fans featuring a wide array of team-related goodies. Fans of the Eastern Conference teams are hardly less passionate than those of the Western Conference so, again, WNBA fandom rookies can find all sorts of lively discussion, trivia tidbits, and fan-friendly content on the Internet (for suggestions see chapter 12).

The following information is current as of the 2007 season.

Juliette Terzieff

Eastern Conference 2007 All-Stars practice session in Washington, D.C.

CHICAGO SKY

Home Venue UIC Pavilion, Chicago, Illinois

Mascot Sky Guy, a Chicago native who used his "jet pack" to fly around the world following basketball before returning home to be a mascot

Team Colors light blue, gold

Owner Michael J. Alter

General Manager Bo Overton

Coach Bo Overton

Team Web site www.wnba.com/sky

Ticket Information Available through team Web site or call 877-329-WBNA

For fans The Sky's Web site has a comprehensive fan guide, photo galleries, a Sky Guy section, sign-up information for the Skywritings e-newsletter, and special game night information.

Fan mail By post: 20 W. Kinzie Street, Suite 1010
Chicago, IL 60610

More about the team: The Chicago Sky made its WNBA debut in the 2006 season, posting five wins throughout the summer schedule. The 2007 season marked a dramatic improvement, as led by team standouts Candice Dupree and Stacey Dales, and new coach Bo Overton. The Sky left the preseason undefeated and made a gallant run at the postseason that would eventually fall short. The Sky's 2007 showing—the team finished 14–20—was a drastic improvement on 2006 for this growing team. Unlike most of the other WNBA teams, the Sky is independent of Chicago's NBA team, the Bulls.

CONNECTICUT SUN

Home Venue	Mohegan Sun Arena, Uncasville, Connecticut
Mascot	Blaze, a shagggy orange creature
Team Colors	blue, red, gold
Owner	The Mohegan Tribe
General Manager	Christopher Sienko
Coach	Mike Thibault
Team Web site	www.connecticutsun.com
Tickets:	Available through team Web site or call 877-SUN-TIXX
For fans	The Sun Web site's fan features include a Blaze Page, a Fan A to Z guide, downloadable wallpapers, e-cards, a page to ask Sun General Manager Christopher Sienko questions, and photo galleries.
Fan mail	By post: Connecticut Sun, ATTN: Fan Mail One Mohegan Sun Boulevard Uncasville, CT 06382

More about the team: The Sun came into being in 2003 as a new incarnation of the Orlando Miracle. It was the first WNBA team not owned by an NBA owner and the only team in a city without an NBA presence. The popularity of women's collegiate basketball, especially the University of Connecticut Huskies, and two former Huskies (Nykesha Sales and Asjha Jones) on the roster, virtually guaranteed the Sun a vociferous home fan base. The Sun marked its territory in the league almost immediately, making a playoff appearance in 2003 before going on to win the Eastern Conference in 2004 and 2005, guaranteeing a trip to the WNBA Championships two years in a row. Though they lost in the finals both times, first to Seattle then to Sacramento, the Sun made their fifth straight playoff appearance in 2007.

DETROIT SHOCK

Home Venue	The Palace of Auburn Hills, Auburn Hills, Michigan
Mascot	Zap, an Australian dingo
Team Colors	blue, red
Owner	William Davidson
General Manager	Bill Laimbeer
Coach	Bill Laimbeer
Team Web site	www.detroitshock.com
Tickets	Available through team Web site or call 248-377-0100
For fans	Fan elements on the Shock Web site include sign-up information for the Shocking News newsletter, a highlights and video section, online contests, downloadable wallpaper, a comprehensive A to Z fan guide, and photo galleries.
Fan mail	By post: Detroit Pistons/Shock
	The Palace of Auburn Hills
	4 Championship Drive
	Auburn Hills, MI 48326

More about the team: The Shock debuted in the league in 1998 as part of the WNBA's first expansion efforts. The team has made it to the playoffs every year since 2003, bringing Detroit the WNBA Championship twice, in 2003 and 2006. After their 2006 championship win, the Shock became the second WNBA team to appear on the cover of a Wheaties cereal box. The Shock charged back into the 2007 WNBA Championship finals, taking the first game against the Phoenix Mercury, with the two combining during the first game for the highest score ever (108–100) in a WNBA finals, but were ultimately unable to repeat their championship winning performance.

INDIANA FEVER

Home Venue	Conseco Fieldhouse, Indianapolis, Indiana
Mascot	Freddy Fever, a big red creature
Team Colors	blue, red, gold
Owner	Herbert and Melvin Simon
General Manager	Kelly Krauskopf
Coach	Brian Winters
Team Web site	www.wnba.com/fever
Tickets	Available through Web site or call 317-917-2500
For fans	The Fever Web site's fan-focused content includes information on how to join the Fever Force Fan Club, photo galleries, desktop wallpapers, and information on special events like the Fever Jr. Hoops Camp.
Fan mail	By post: Conseco Fieldhouse
	One Conseco Court
	125 S. Pennsylvania Street
	Indianapolis, IN 46204

More about the team: The Fever debuted in the 2000 WNBA season alongside Seattle, Portland, and Miami as part of the league's expansion efforts. Indiana made its first playoff appearance in 2002, and returned in 2004, 2005, and 2007 led by teammates Tamika Catchings and Tully Bevilaqua. The 2007 season, which saw the additions of veterans Sheri Sam and Tammy Sutton-Brown to the team roster, saw the Fever surpass numerous milestones, including becoming the first team in WNBA history to win at least twenty games three years in a row, achieving the best start (16–4) in Eastern Conference history, and post the largest postseason comeback in WNBA history, overcoming a deficit of twenty-two points to beat the Sun.

NEW YORK LIBERTY

Home Venue	Madison Square Garden, New York, New York
Mascot	Maddie, the dog
Team Colors	blue, orange, liberty (sea foam) green
Owner	Cablevision
General Manager	Carol Blazejowski
Coach	Pat Coyle
Team Web site	www.wnba.com/liberty
Tickets	Available on team Web site or call 212-465-6073
For fans	The Liberty Web site has extensive fan-related material, including sign-up information for the Liberty e-news and Liberty Summer Basketball Camp, downloadable wallpaper, message boards, and a comprehensive Inside the Key guide to basketball playing and coaching basics.
Fan mail	By post: New York Liberty 2 Pennsylvania Plaza New York, NY 10121

More about the team: One of the original eight WNBA teams, the New York Liberty shared center stage with the Los Angeles Sparks in the first-ever WNBA game in Los Angeles on June 21, 1997, emerging victorious with a 67–57 win. The Liberty has made more appearances at the WNBA Championships than any other in the Eastern Conference and ties the Houston Comets for the most—four—appearances. While the Comets won the finals in four back-to-back appearances, the Liberty has yet to bring home the championship. Even though the Liberty have not made it back to the big show since 2002, they are considered one of the main contenders in the Eastern Conference and remain a regular feature of postseason play. Through the 2007 season, 1998 and 2003 are the only years the Liberty did not make a playoff appearance.

WASHINGTON MYSTICS

Home Venue	Verizon Center, Washington, D.C.
Mascot	Pax, the panda
Team Colors	blue, black, bronze
Owner	Lincoln Holdings, LLC (Sheila Johnson)
General Manager	Linda Hargrove
Coach	Wayne "Tree" Rollins (interim)
Team Web site:	www.wnba.com/mystics/
Tickets	Available through team Web site or call 877-DC-HOOP1
For fans	The Mystics' Web site has information for fans on Mystics Basketball camps and community events, downloadable wallpaper, and game video highlights.
Fan mail	By post: Verizon Center
	601 F Street, NW
	Washington, D.C. 20004

More about the team: The Mystics began league play in the 1998 season as one of the WNBA's first expansion teams, and have made several appearances in the WBNA playoffs (2000, 2002, 2004, and 2006). The Mystics 2007 season got off to a particularly rough start, with the team going 0–8 before the surprise departure of Head Coach Richie Adubato. Longtime basketball fixture Wayne "Tree" Rollins stepped in and helped the team capitalize on the presence of prolific scorers Alana Beard, Monique Curry, and DeLisha Milton-Jones on their way to a 17W–20L season tally.

SIX

Playing the Game

Even those who have never taken an interest in the finer points of basketball can give at least a rudimentary explanation of the game. But for those who are on their way to joining the ranks of the WNBA or NCAA fan base, "bounce the ball, put in the basket" just doesn't quite cut it. For those new to the game, here is a brief discussion of the tools and basic skills involved, which WNBA legend Kym Hampton helped create (for a bit more, take a look at our basketball glossary, pp. 173–176). For those readers already well versed in hoops lingo, it's a nice little reference package for your newbie friends, with a few surprises thrown in.

BASKETBALL BASICS

In its most basic configuration, basketball is understood to involve two teams, each with five players on the court; each side tasked with placing the basketball into the opposite (opposing team's) basket more frequently than the opposing team. The five players—two forwards, a center, and two guards—are responsible not only for a team's offense but its defense as well (see later in this chapter for more detailed discussion of the various roles players fulfill). In the WNBA, each team's season roster contains eleven players, five of them making up the starting lineup—or core group of players who will begin almost every game on the court. The most important player on the roster following the starting lineup is the so-called sixth man (in this case, woman)—who will be the first substitute to enter the game. Officials may assess fouls against a player for illegal interference or play, and any player who accrues six fouls in a game is automatically removed from the active lineup for the rest of the game.

In the case of the WNBA, as per 2007 season guidelines which follow rules almost identical to the NBA, the game is played in two halves, divided into four, ten-minute quarters. The visiting team gets to choose which basket it would prefer for the first half. Teams change target baskets at the half, and any overtime is played as an extension of the second half. Should the allotted regular game time end with both teams equal in score, the game will move to overtime periods, five minutes in length and as many as necessary, until one team outscores the other.

TOOLS

The court itself is 94 feet long by 50 feet wide, and once in possession of the ball a team on offense has eight seconds to cross the mid-court line, which during play delineates offensive and defensive playing areas, and a total of twenty-four seconds to get off a shot on the basket. The free throw line (see Scoring below) is mandated to be located 15 feet from the backboard. The three point line (see Scoring) travels from the edge of the court from the baseline 63 inches in an elongated arc of 20 feet, 6.25 inches toward the mid-court line, with its side boundaries set at 54 inches from both sidelines.

The basket has an 18-inch diameter with a net 15 to 18 inches long, while the ball itself should have a circumference of 29.5–30 inches.

SKILLS

Like any sport, basketball has a core list of fundamental skills, in this case involving dribbling, passing, and shooting, which any player must master if she hopes to play professionally.

The uncontested central skill in basketball is *dribbling*. A player and her team cannot move down the court without it, and unless the opposing team decides to hand off the ball beneath the basket every time, no team can win without moving the ball up and down the court.

Simply put, dribbling is the ability to bounce the ball off the floor up and down the court. In basketball, a player cannot run, walk, or otherwise move in any direction laterally while in possession of the ball if she is not dribbling. There is no limit to the number of times a player can dribble the ball (besides the obvious time crunch of the twenty-four-second scoring rule and opposing players breathing down one's neck), and a dribble comes to an end when the player in possession of the ball either places both hands on the ball or holds the ball. At that point, the player cannot begin to dribble anew without having first passed the ball to another player, taken a shot, or having lost and regained possession. Any player who takes more than two steps when receiving the ball and has not begun to dribble is charged with traveling; any player who stops a dribble and begins again without meeting the above criteria is charged with a double dribble. In both cases, the player's team will lose possession of the ball.

The *pivot*, in which the player cements one foot (then the pivot foot) to the floor and turns, fakes a step, or otherwise seeks to outwit defenders by moving only the second foot, is a central element to finding an open shot or passing lane to a teammate and can be used at the end of a dribble, recovery of a rebound, or as part of a passing offensive tactic.

Passing is the main method of getting the ball from one player to another (although a player may seize the ball away from opponents via steals or rebounds). A *chest pass*, in which a player passes the ball from chest height in a fairly straight line, is most often employed when there is an open passing lane opportunity to a teammate. Several types of passes, such as the *bounce pass*, in which a player bounces a ball under or past a defender, are employed when opposing players are in close vicinity on defending. Like the bounce pass, the *give-and-go*—in which a player passes and makes a quick break for the basket in time to receive a return pass—is a standard offensive evasive maneuver. The overhead pass can be used to soar over the heads of defenders to reach an open teammate, but is most often used following a rebound to make an overhead outlet pass to a teammate near mid-court, aimed at starting a fast break toward the basket in the hopes of getting off a successful shot before the opposing team has time to get back into a defensive formation.

Rebounding can be an offensive or defensive move, depending on who comes down with the ball after an unsuccessful attempt at a basket, but is central to the overall game. Nobody shoots 100 percent all of the time, and a successful offense is one that can grab a wayward shot and convert it for another attempt, or two, or three, at the basket until the team puts points up on the scoreboard. For the defense, rebounding is key for the same reason, because it signals a new offensive opportunity for that player's team (and more chances to score) while denying opponents the chance to take more shots and score. A quick grab by a defensive player can also lead to a quick outlet pass and perhaps a shot at the basket before the other team can rally its defense.

SCORING

A basket can be worth one, two, or three points depending on the location on the court from which the shot originates and whether the shot occurs during regular play or as part of an assessed penalty.

A basket scored during regular play can be worth two or three points, depending on whether the shot is taken from inside or outside the three-point line. In the WNBA, the three-point line travels up from the baseline, 54 inches in from the sidelines, back behind the free throw area, to an arced point that is over 20 feet from the basket. Any successful shot taken from outside the three-point line is worth three points.

Two-point shots, those taken from inside or on the three-point line, can be any number of standard basketball shots, including jump shots, dunks, rebounded put-backs, baby hooks, finger rolls, and layups (see Glossary).

A free throw is worth one point per successful shot and is pretty much what the name implies, in that a free throw shot is taken free from any attempt by the defensive team to block, intercept, or otherwise interfere with the ball before it hits the rim. Free throw attempts must be taken from the free throw line, which is a standard 15 feet from the basket's backboard, and are awarded as the result of a personal foul by one player on another of the opposing team. Depending on the infraction involved, a player may be awarded up to three free throw attempts.

Technical fouls can include illegal contact with another player, such as unsportsmanlike elbow contact, delay of game, and coaching staff members or teammates on the bench leaving their allotted space on the floor. According to the accepted standard rules of the game, a personal foul can include any contact that is deemed to involve holding onto, pushing, or accidental charging into another player. Those who are assessed technical fouls for unsportsmanlike conduct in the league also face monetary fines and potential suspensions for each infraction.

SCHEDULING

The WNBA season officially kicks off in mid-May following a two-week preseason, during which teams will play preparatory games against opponents they'll meet in the regular season. The short preseason is intended to give teams and their coaching staff time to configure their final lineups for the season, run rookie players through their paces, and give players time to acclimate to one another ahead of the fast-paced summer season.

In the short span of time between mid-May and mid-August, each team will play thirty-four regular games, meeting teams from both within and

IN THEIR OWN WORDS

VAN CHANCELLOR

For those who follow women's basketball, Van Chancellor is a household name. Chancellor was the last of the original coaches to leave the league, which he did after the 2006 season to return to the collegiate game. When he decided to leave the Houston Comets he did so with an unrivaled four straight consecutive WNBA Championships wins, three WNBA Coach of the Year Awards, a 211–111 ten-year game record, and an induction into the Basketball Hall of Fame. Chancellor, now head coach of the women's program at Louisiana State University, spoke about some of his secrets to winning, particularly in the postseason.

The true secret to winning is a combination of having those great players and creating the situations where they can showcase their skills. You have to know what your players can do and draw up the plays to reflect that. That involves going to each individual player and discussing her role—starting with the shooters first and asking them "where do you want the ball?" and then getting the other players to accept their roles. In professional play there will always be individual players who are "stars" or who stand out, and that can be a challenge for other team members, but at the end of the day the players want to win.

outside their conference, in the hopes of compiling a strong enough record to get them through to the postseason and a run at their conference championship and on to the WNBA Championship.

Teams that qualify for postseason play get about one week between the end of the regular season and the postseason's start. Three weeks later, one

For the postseason the place you have to start is with the knowledge that you've made it and then work to make sure not to let the pressure get to you or your players. What the team needs to do is relax and play their game.

We would go through all the regular season games with teams we'd face in the postseason and look for spots where we had trouble, where someone was reading our defense, or where a defensive player was getting particularly good reads on our offense, and then work on adjusting our play around those trouble spots. For example, in 2000, Tameka Dixon was doing a superb job of penetrating and Los Angeles had beaten us three times in a row. We had to find a way to adjust around that in order to win.

Favorite Play: The "C." It's a simple play involving a side screen and a roll, with one player on the wing shooting from the outside. Simple enough play, but when you've got the players it just works.

of the teams participating in postseason play will lift the WNBA Championship trophy and stake its place in the record books.

COACHING AND STRATEGY

Now at first glance, this would seem easy enough. Tell your players to maintain possession of the ball by any legal means necessary, drive down the court, and sink it into the basket more times than your opponent. Of course if it was that easy anyone with even a smidge of interest in sports would be out there coaching championship teams every year.

"Coaching is not about basketball, it's about people," says Clay Kallam, creator of the Web-based basketball information clearinghouse Full Court Press (see chapter 12) and longtime high school girls' basketball coach. "Whether to play man-to-man or zone, setting screens, or fronting the post . . . those are all details. It's the group dynamic, the belief that the team will succeed, that wins games."

A WNBA coaching staff deals with players of various experience levels, from rookies straight out of college to women who have competed at the pinnacle of women's worldwide basketball for years. With a short preseason, coaches must make sure the women on their roster play well together by identifying the key partnerships and also help players who may not have ever played together before rapidly develop team cohesiveness. With new players coming into and retiring from the league every year, coaches are often faced with the need to foretell the best, and worst, matchups their players will face in the regular season and prepare them accordingly.

Among their other key decisions, of course, is the development of plays and team strategies, and under which conditions to implement them. Coaching staff must also play multiple interpersonal roles, including disciplinarian, task master, nurturer, friend, and teacher to players as they face the ups and downs of playing highly competitive professional sports.

POSITIONS AND ROLES

The fast-paced movement of players and the ball around the basketball court as teams battle for points and switch strategies and players can—to the uninitiated—make it appear as though the game is a bit of a free-for-all. Truth is, the manic pace of the game couldn't be upheld without concentrated teamwork based on a set of ground rules for the various players and the role they assume during the game. Traditionally, a basketball team's on-court presence is mapped out around five positions—a point guard, shooting guard, power forward, small forward, and the center. While each of the positions carries its own scope of responsibility and demands expertise in certain skill sets, players must always be prepared to step forward, or back, to make a play or fill a hole on either defense or offense. Many players excel in areas traditionally outside the scope of their position; over the last few decades, such skills have led to hybrid positions like guard-forward and forward-center.

As the game has evolved, so have the players, and the results can be astounding. Take a look at relatively tiny Tully Bevilaqua as she prowls down the court in full command, Candice Dupree when she steals the ball and races down the court like she has jet engines attached to her feet, or Penny Miller as she commands an offense like a five-star general. The skills and talent of WNBA players are prodigious, and even though they may make it all look easy, the results would not be possible if each and every player didn't know exactly what role her team depends on her to fill.

Guards

While the extent of the *point guard* role may change slightly based on a team's overall coaching strategy, experience of the player involved, and the balance of skills on the team as a whole, the point guard is, literally, point person number one on the court; *the* playmaker on the court directing the offense and its tempo. Working in close cooperation with the coaching staff, the point guard knows which strategies, formations, and plays to call during a game and is often referred to as "coach on the floor."

Head up and driving upcourt in search of an opportunity, the point guard—perhaps more than any other player on the court—must be a master of the "no look" and "fake" passes to beat defenders off the ball. Speed, both physical and mental, and fierce ball handling skills, are keys to a point guard's success. Knowing when to pass, how to get your team to open up, and when to back the ball up giving teammates a chance to get into better scoring positions are among the many decisions a point guard will face in a typical game.

A point guard also needs to know the individual strengths of her team-

KATIE DOUGLAS

Connecticut Sun guard-forward Katie Douglas has built a solid reputation as a prolific scorer since joining the league in 2001, with multiple appearances in the WNBA Playoffs and All-Star Games. Douglas, selected as a starting shooting guard for the 2007 All-Star Game, sat down to talk about a shooting guard's responsibilities and the pure grit that's gotten her to this level.

The position: A player must have fierce scoring skills in this position. Look to help your team make shots by identifying opportunities, matchups that can be beat for points . . . help point guards by creating opportunities. Make sure stand-still and quick-shooting abilities are strengths.

Every possession means the possibility of a different defensive posture, so quick instincts and response are vital. Beware of defensive players trying to throw you off your individual rhythm; have a prepared strategy to get around the play when others are trying to knock you off your game.

mates and the matchups they're facing in order to best place the ball for scoring opportunities. For example, if a point guard's team has other players who represent a dominant scoring threat, the point guard may sit back a little and emphasize assists while making sure the scorers get their chances to put up points on the scoreboard. At the same time, a point guard also needs to be a strong scoring contender and know when best to take her shots so that the opposing team doesn't move its defense off her to block or double team other offensive players.

To see the magic a professional point guard creates on the courts, check out the game moves of WNBA stars, including Tully Bevilaqua, Sue Bird, Penny Miller, or Ticha Penichiero.

Her favorite move(s): Everyone knows I love the left side and the pick and roll is one of my favorite moves.

Her inspirations: My family.

Her challenges: Everyone faces challenges. For me, it was the loss of my parents at a very young age. It was devastating, and a loss you never truly get over. But if you have strong family and friends around you it helps you work forward. I continue to wish my parents were here, that they could see me now . . . I know they would be very proud. [Note: Douglas tragically lost both her parents to cancer in a three-year period.]

Tips for success: Never think you have to stop working to get better. Keep working on key elements, like footwork, quick response times, and stand-still shooting.

A *shooting guard*'s main responsibility, as the name implies, is to score, score, score. A player in this position is looked to by her teammates as someone who can score from anywhere on the court, and who is able to read a defense effectively and create her own scoring opportunities. Stand still and jump shots, a ferocious drive to the basket, and a consistently successful ability to catch-and-shoot (receive a pass, set up and release a zinger quickly, and score), are the domain of the shooting guard. Players in this position should be good ball handlers and passers though these skills are not their primary focus points.

Great shooting guards maintain a high percentage from outside the

IN THEIR OWN WORDS

DELISHA MILTON-JONES

Washington Mystics forward DeLisha "Sunshine" Milton-Jones, who began her WNBA career as the "silent assassin" for the Los Angeles Sparks, has amassed an impressive WNBA resume that includes multiple All-Star and WNBA Playoffs appearances, as well as a 2001 WNBA Championship. Milton-Jones graciously took time to speak about what being a championship caliber forward entails and her secrets for success.

The position: A forward needs to be versatile, the kind of player who can get inside the paint and mix it up, put the ball to the court, and shoot well from the outside. A forward has to be good at every single basketball skill to compete successfully.

Her favorite move(s): Easy. . . . Layups, layups, layups.

Her inspirations: My grandparents, who were instrumental in teaching me the importance of determination and perseverance. Coaches who urged me forward and helped me build upon the early lessons from my family.

three-point line—in other words, an ever-present perimeter threat—when on offense, that provides pivotal game-changing points while also serving a secondary, but often critical, purpose to draw out the opposing team's defense and open up lanes to the basket.

To see the scoring prowess of a professional shooting guard, look to WNBA stars Betty Lennox, Seimone Augustus, Tan White, Diana Taurasi, and Nykesha Sales.

And other players . . . when you play against people like Tina Thompson, Tamika Catchings, or Lisa Leslie, well, they're the best of the best and they elevate your level of playing; you have to bring your "A" game if you want to compete with matchups like those.

Her challenges: Coming back from my ACL (knee ligament) injury. Bouncing back after an injury is harder than you would think if you have not experienced it, but with a strong sense of determination and a very good support network you can do it.

Tips for success: You have got to have patience. Watch a lot of basketball, and keep a particular eye on those playing the position you prefer and the matchups that occur. Take your time and learn one skill at a time to become a well-rounded player. And take care of yourself. If you eat right and pay attention to the little things in your life you can play as long as you like.

Forwards

A *power forward*, ironically enough, plays much of her close quarters offense facing backward—away from the basket—and scores most of her points from the low post, or less than six feet away from the basket. Known for their size and strength, power forwards are looked to as creative rebounders and defenders, and are also likely to be found in the low post area when on defense, ready to snag a rebound for their team. In other words, the power forward is usually the chief rebounder on both ends of the court.

With their positioning so close to the basket, the power forward, natu-

IN THEIR OWN WORDS

TAMMY SUTTON-BROWN

Since joining the WNBA in 2001 as the second Canadian-born player ever to be drafted, Sutton-Brown led the Charlotte Sting in blocks and became the first Canadian player selected as an All-Star, before moving on to the Indiana Fever before the 2007 season. Sutton-Brown sat down on the sidelines ahead of her 2007 All-Star Game appearance to talk about being a world class center and what it takes to mix it up with the WNBA's best players.

The position: You have to be aggressive both defensively and on offense. You are the last line of defense if someone else is getting beat. Get in the paint, block the shots, and pursue the rebounds . . . pressure, pressure, pressure the opponent.

Her favorite move(s): Reading a defense and reacting quickly; it's a thrill when it goes right.

Her inspirations: A lot of people helped me along the way, my parents

rally, is often found to be in the best position to begin a fast break for her team: recovering the ball and completing a quick outlet pass to a teammate to set up the score.

Big-time WNBA power forwards include Rebekkah Brunson, Cheryl Ford, Catherine Kraayeveld, and Tina Thompson.

The *small forward* is the *everyman* (or in this case *woman*) of the team, an extremely versatile player who is expected to put points up on the scoreboards on offense, and simultaneously be able to block well, pass efficiently, and be the second line rebound-recovery specialist behind the power forward on defense. The position's name is deceiving, as a small forward needs

especially, but coaches who really cared too, and all of that love, it stays with you, motivates you.

Her challenges: Thankfully I've had no major injuries so far in my career because those can be extremely tough to overcome. For me, I think one of the hardest things I've faced was leaving home to go off to [Rutgers] university . . . yes, there was some loneliness and fear then, but looking back I wouldn't trade it for anything.

Tips for success: It may sound incredibly basic but it is true: practice. Never think that you are going to be perfect, know that you will always have to practice, and then practice some more, if you want to stay in the game . . . For everything you achieve there is always more out there to reach for, a goal you have yet to meet.

to be big and able to play both an inside or outside game equally well. Size is paramount for the small forward to carve a path through defenders to the basket and for battling rebounds.

Small forwards each have their own individual ways of scoring points, but generally display a particular aptitude for getting "to the line"—in other words, drawing a foul from a defensive player when attempting close-quarter shots at the basket. As a result, accurate foul-line shooting is a key skill for the small forward.

Established small forwards in the WNBA include Svetlana Abrosimova, Tamika Catchings, Iziane Castro Marques, Sheryl Swoopes, and Sophia Young.

The *guard/forward* is a player with demonstrable ability to play both the small forward and shooting guard positions effectively against most match-ups. With the size and strength necessary for the small forward position, combined with the outside jump shot and speed of the shooting guard, the hybrid players—such as Alana Beard, Deanna Nolan, Ticha Penichiero, and Nykesha Sales—can cause real defensive headaches for the opposing team.

Centers

Just about any quest for success in life requires one to maintain balance, to be centered and focused on the goal. Winning a basketball game is no different and on the court that role is filled, as the name suggests, by the *center*. Traditionally the tallest player on the team, centers must have a dominating presence in the paint and are usually the team's primary low-post scorer. They are also primarily responsible for anchoring a team's play on defense and rebounding both offensively and defensively.

WNBA stars like Margo Dydek, Yolanda Griffith, Lisa Leslie, Janel Mc-Carville, and Ruth Riley are some prime examples of championship caliber centers.

Like the guard/forward, the *forward/center* is a hybrid position for those players who have played the power forward and center positions on a consistently successful basis. Taken individually the positions require different skill sets, but the two overlap, particularly in rebounding and passing. A power forward, for example, is often a fiercely capable inside defender, a role the center is also expected to perform. Players who have demonstrated their ability to fill both roles include Lauren Jackson, Tangela Smith, Taj McWilliams-Franklin, and Asjha Jones.

SEVEN

Cultural Impact

U nlike virtually any other societal element, sports has the uncanny ability to unite people from across racial, economic, political, and social boundaries toward a common purpose. Its stars are national—and often international—heroes prized primarily for the admirable qualities of talent combined with hard work and dedication. Historically the heroes of sports have been overwhelmingly male, but women athletes have worked hard to stake out a place for themselves in sports and American pop culture in recent decades that can only benefit both men *and* women. As a league in one of the most widely played, watched, and admired sports in America, the WNBA's survival into a second decade (and beyond . . .) marks not only a victory for women's sports aficionados but for American culture as a whole as we move further into the twenty-first century.

The popularity of the game of basketball is undeniable. From the decrepit, inner-city playgrounds of America's teeming metropolises to the glittering, history-filled hall of Madison Square Garden, basketball is—perhaps more than any other sport—the great equalizer; the game any boy or girl with a ball can play anywhere, anytime. No fancy equipment is needed; no special training either; just passion, passion, and more passion. To go the distance as a professional athlete you need an extremely healthy dose of talent, grit, and sheer determination. And as most Americans have played basketball (at the very least as part of PE classes in elementary school), as a whole we understand that spectacular results a la Cynthia Cooper, Lisa Leslie, or Diana Taurasi deserve our cheers.

Women's participation in sports, as discussed earlier in the book, is certainly nothing new, but the cultural changes that began in earnest just a few decades ago have led to opportunities and changes once thought unachievable. Evidence of the successes associated with these changes can be seen in the WNBA, the increased television and advertising dollars allotted for the NCAA tournament, WNBA game broadcasting, and multimillion, multi-year deals for female athletes with major corporate sponsors. Just eight years ago, as the world marked a new century, few NCAA games were available to television viewers and endorsement deals from sponsors for females were few and far between.

And while the changes are occurring even as you read, it will take decades to fully appreciate the true and full cultural contribution that the WNBA makes to American society and the youngsters now dreaming of following in their heroes' footsteps.

In the last couple of decades, male sports have been plagued by a rash of scandals that have left many fans—especially women—with a sour taste in their mouths. From Mike Tyson to Kobe Bryant, Michael Vick to Barry Bonds, allegations of sexual assault, drug use, and a host of other illegal activities have shone powerful spotlights on the lives of major sports stars, away from the sports field of battle. Beyond emotional knee-jerk reactions of repulsion, massive and sometimes inaccurate or presumptuous reporting, and ugly legal proceedings, guilt or innocence has often taken a backseat to public perception—which can be particularly damning for anyone involved in such cases, and to the sports world at large.

Juliette Terzieff

Monique Currie engages with WNBA BE Tour participants in Washington, D.C.

With conviction rates for male athletes far lower than the national average (around 30 percent as compared to more than 60 percent), many believe this is part and parcel of a sports culture that values investment in an athlete more than an athlete's nonsports behavior. Millions of dollars are invested into the grooming, training, and marketing of players for premier sports leagues, and public perception is that athletes—like many actors and actresses—often reap the benefits of "celebrity justice."

Female athletes—with the notable exceptions of athletes such as sprinter Marion Jones and figure skater Tonya Harding—have not faced the kind of criminal and legal woes that plague their male counterparts, providing an alternative place for disgruntled sports fans to turn. While male sports stars have come to be viewed with a certain level of suspicion and distrust as role models in some quarters of American society, female sports figures to many young women and their parents represent a different model than the men; a more positive, healthy example.

Female athletes have further advantages over other contemporary role models. Most cover girls in the fashion world are often uberskinny and even unhealthy looking, while athletes by comparison are often thin with a low percentage of body fat but obviously in good health. Like models, most actresses are extremely skinny and, in youth-obsessed Hollywood, prone to having multiple cosmetic surgeries to alter their looks. While female athletes are no strangers to being marketed for their outer beauty, in part to placate a lingering ambivalence toward female athletes in popular American culture, the picture they present is one of all-around well-being and the result of healthy living. For parents, the emergence of health-centered role models is a welcome alternative to the unattainable standard of "magazine cover" beauty that other industries promote.

Among the athletic community, the mass popularity of the sport of basketball affords WNBA players a greater chance to reach more young men and women than female athletic stars like Mia Hamm, Michelle Kwan, or golfer Michelle Wie. No slights intended to fans of soccer, figure skating, or golf, but those sports simply do not have the kind of mass appeal of America's premier sports: football, basketball, baseball, and hockey. As a consequence, while figure skating is a much-loved sport that attracts plenty of publicity in Olympic years, as does soccer around the same time and for World Cups, and golf certainly has a large following, stars in these sports simply do not have the comparable staying power of basketball stars in the public eye.

Of the four main dominant American sports, only basketball has a professional league for women. Hockey does have rather admirable amateur and university-level opportunities. Female football play, in stark comparison, has not taken off at any level despite the passion of a relatively small core group of players that emerges in each successive generation. As for baseball, young women looking to play are encouraged to play softball instead (though there are those who believe that the best chance for female players to play in a male league is in baseball, rather than hockey, basketball, or football).

With the WNBA's deal in place to extend the broadcasting of most of its games on the ABC network and ESPN through 2016, the players will continue to have a relatively high profile in the summer. That deal, announced in July 2007, was a major endorsement from the sports broadcasting world of its confidence that the WNBA will continue to expand its sphere of influence among sports fans in the coming years. The exposure benefits associated with major broadcasting outlets cannot be overstated, not the least of which is the increase in revenue the league and its players hope to gain in the future.

The world of American sports is witnessing the beginning stages of a shift toward greater recognition through endorsement deals for female players that were, as recently as the turn of the century eight years ago, the almost exclusive domain of male stars. Much of the shift is likely the result of consistently growing numbers of women watching and playing sports, and corporations desire to cater to this growing demographic group. Today. female athletes like Maria Sharapova and Michelle Wie place in the top ten on *Forbes* magazine's list of the top earning superstars under twenty-five (actors, singers, athletes, and entrepreneurs) based on their 2006 to 2007 earnings,* but no female athlete made an appearance on *Sports Illustrated*'s 2007 top fifty earning American athletes. Earnings from salary and endorsements are by no means the sole measure of an individual's talent, but are a reflection of their marketability as perceived by investors. That women have begun to make appearances on many of the tracking lists demonstrates their increasing inclusion in the top tier of sports superstars with staying power.

---

*"20 Under 25: The Top-Earning Young Superstars"; Forbes, December 4, 2007.

With the relatively small salaries earned by WNBA players (as compared to those in tournament winnings–producing sports such as tennis and golf), it will be some time before any of them crack open that particular barrier, but that doesn't mean the endorsements and support aren't also beginning to materialize for these hardworking ladies.

Many women's sports aficionados believe the ability of the WNBA to survive, and thrive, into and past the two-decade threshold—not forgetting the strong presence of leagues including the Ladies Professional Golf Association and the Women's Tennis Association—may actively contribute to the proliferation of more professional woman's sport leagues in the years to come. The LPGA, which was formed by a group of thirteen women that included Babe Didrikson Zacharias, has been arranging sporting events since the 1960s, while the WTA came into being in the early 1970s. The WNBA will be looking to build upon their longevity and notable successes—and others are also looking to follow suit. A new professional soccer league, initially named the Women's Soccer LLC, is set to begin play in spring 2009 with teams in cities including Boston, Chicago, Denver, and Los Angeles. As for the WNBA, it also has plans to expand, with the first announcement coming in October 2007 that a new team based in Atlanta, Georgia, would begin play in the 2008 season. There has been plenty of buzz surrounding other potential expansion moves with New Jersey, Florida, Colorado, and Utah thrown around as possibilities, as well as a bit of perhaps far-fetched talk about expanding the league to include play from some Canadian teams after 2010. Whatever the particulars of professional basketball and soccer expansion efforts that eventually come to pass, the growing ability of women's professional leagues to thrive in the United States is a testament to the changing face of American pop culture and the new spaces into which women are making headway.

EIGHT

Fan Factor

To be a WNBA fan is to be a member of a close-knit community of people from around the country. With such a relatively small number of teams in relation to others sports like men's basketball, hockey, and baseball, fans are often spread across wide geographical areas, but that hardly keeps them from sharing their passion online through Web sites and fan forums. Fans will go ahead and arrange their own draft day parties, All-Star dinners, and other get-togethers to coincide with WNBA events that draw in fans from different areas. They write poems and create fan Web sites; make homemade banners for the games; and avidly collect player cards, jerseys, and autographs.

As obvious as fan love for the players, the game, and the league is, the WNBA has had mixed success in engaging the two biggest groups in its core fan base—families and the gay and lesbian community—despite their presence in the stands being vital to the league's survival. But whatever the difficulties of the association—including the occasional public grumbling from fans—any talk of giving up on the relationship is met universally with derision. WNBA fans are no less than an extended family that is extremely protective of the league and its players. Given the troubled past of women's professional basketball leagues in the United States, many fans truly believe that the WNBA is *the* last, best chance for a league with staying power.

Families, especially those with young girls, have found themselves actively courted by the league through initiatives like the "Dads & Daughters" program. Under the program, each team hosts a Dads & Daughters night during a home game, with incentives like special ticket prices, contests, and giveaways. Teams also host a variety of theme nights throughout the season, including Moms and Kids Nights, Kids Days, and Fan Appreciation Days. Family friendly entertainment is always on hand at WNBA games, from jugglers and magicians that prowl the Chicago arena concourse, to the Los Angeles Sparks SparKids dance group of eight- to thirteen-year-olds and the New York Liberty's Timeless Torches dancers, all of whom are over forty.

Ticket prices remain extremely reasonable for a professional sporting event, with many of the teams offering heavily discounted season, six-game discount, or family packages. For the price of one single ticket to a National Football League or National Basketball Association game an entire family can go and see a WNBA game. And unlike a movie, play, or other cultural events that families can enjoy together, a WNBA game carries little of the inappropriate content concerns for parents associated with other opportunities, and is a blood-pumping interactive experience for all.

When it comes to the rub, though, for families the appeal of the league is not so much a matter of the family-friendly side entertainments or inexpensive tickets prices as it is the mutual love and respect the players and their young female fans can share. For mothers and fathers, the women of the WNBA provide a great opportunity to show their young daughters what it means to chase a dream that might not be considered "mainstream."

"These women are not making a lot of money but they're still putting out incredible effort to build the league. They have college degrees, work hard, and are polite," says David Siegel, a Farmington, Connecticut, father of a preteen girl. "The way players interact with the kids has been phenomenal.

They don't talk to them like they are kids, but relate to them like they are little people, and that has been extremely important for my daughter."

Siegel's daughter Danielle has literally grown up with the WNBA, learning "how to shake someone's hand and look them in the eye." Danielle has a massive collection of autographed WNBA and player memorabilia she personally collected, the family dog is named Whalen (after Lindsey), and the family gets to spend solid blocks of time together doing something they can all enjoy.

It may sound a bit cliché but for the tens of thousands of WNBA fans, that happy family picture has been the charm of this young league. Little girls talking hoops with their professional heroes, the older crowd hanging out at the local watering hole after the game, players knowing fans by sight and by name—that sense of community, any longtime WNBA fan will swear, has been the magic of the league.

It's an enchantment that goes both ways. For many players engaging with the fans is a reaffirmation of the struggles they've faced in trying to reach the upper levels of women's professional sports.

"My hoops heroes were Larry Bird and Dr. J, and I could only watch one women's game a year on television, the championships," Rebecca Lobo says of her pre-WNBA childhood. "It's great now for young girls and boys that the 'W' exists, and they can see that it is good and 'normal' for girls to play sports. Both young boys and young girls need to understand that."

During Lobo's years with the New York Liberty, she often encountered a young girl who would wait outside the arena to walk the legendary forward inside for the games. They developed a friendship that would continue beyond Lobo's move from New York and 2003 retirement from the league to the present day.

"She is now a twenty-year-old woman who I consider a friend of mine. I watched her grow up and I'm proud that the league existed for kids like [her]," Lobo says.

But part of the problem with the happy family picture the league has tried to create is that one of the members has been allowed only a grudging spot at the very end of the table—the gay and lesbian community. No major sports league has actively courted this community in an open, consistent manner, so few are truly surprised by the league's stance (especially with a growing marketing emphasis on gaining corporate sponsors rather than gaining fans), but all the same, as America's preeminent professional female major sports league, many within the gay and lesbian community had hoped for more.

In the early days of the league, several teams hosted gay-and-lesbian-friendly events in bids to openly court the base. The Seattle Storm took out ads in gay publications, organized a Gay Pride night at one of their 2000-season home games, and gave away blocks of tickets to community groups. The Sparks attended a "Gay Pride Kickoff" party at one of the country's largest women's dance clubs in 2001 to a rapturous welcome from the community and applause from Los Angelinos in general. But while some teams embraced the fan base, others lashed out, refusing to post the names of gay and lesbian groups on the overhead scoreboard alongside other groups that bought blocks of tickets, or insisting fans refrain from holding openly gay and lesbian signage at the games. As the league approached the anniversary of its first decade, the emphasis shifted heavily away from recognizing the gay and lesbian fan base.

"All you have to do is walk into an arena hosting a WNBA game and look around the stands to see the community represented," says Full Court Press creator Clay Kallam. "There were surely some families who objected in the early days, but any families now coming to games have come to terms with it and are comfortable with it."

The unofficial "don't ask, don't tell" policy has, of course, affected players even more deeply than it has fans, forcing them into the stereotype of the "athlete-mother" that may not actually represent their lifestyle. For both gay and straight players it is a brutally unfair situation that has forced teammates to circle the wagons to protect a secret the vast majority feel no need to keep and one that isn't really a secret at all. Indeed, anyone who follows the game for even just a few months can rattle off the names of bi- or homosexual players—everyone knows, and nobody really seems to feel it makes any hoot of a difference to the players' games or their individual contributions to the sport.

Many argue the league has come to the realization that in-arena attendance, which averaged just over 10,000 people per game in 1999 but dropped steadily over the years to less than 7,500 in 2006, is unlikely to change significantly over the next few years and that the big money needed to run and grow the league will come from corporate sponsors. While it may or may not be a realistic assessment of the politics of corporate sponsorship, the league seems to have adopted the attitude that many potential sponsors would be unlikely to support the league if it openly embraced its homosexual players.

Many gay and lesbian fans chafe at the apparently purposeful exclusion of the community from the WNBA marketing plan, arguing that as the community is such a natural and vital component of the fan base it deserves more respect. "Basically, the message being sent is 'we want your money, but we don't want you'," one die-hard fan says of the league's attitude. For others though, the aversion to publicly embracing such a political issue when the league is trying to establish itself is understandable and necessary.

"It would be interesting if the league would take an ethical, moral stand to be proud of the players and who they are," Kallam believes.

Whatever the politics associated with the league and the teams' gay and lesbian fans, the community, like WNBA fans as a whole, remains dedicated to the success of the rookie women's basketball league.

With the WNBA being a women's league in an arena—sports—that has been dominated by men since the earliest organized sporting event in history (the 776 B.C. Olympic Games), no discussion of WNBA fandom would be complete without a quick shout-out to the male fans. Many of them have come to the league drawn by curiosity, a love of basketball in general, or, like many of the female fans, to follow players as they graduated out of the NCAA into the professional arena. Women make up about 75 percent of the

WNBA's in-arena fan presence, but the WNBA's male fans are equally passionate about the game. Many of the fan Web sites were created by men and some of the WNBA's most productive bloggers are males.

The following poem, written by WNBA fanatic Stephen Burt, shows that passion for the women's game can cut across any remaining societal perceptions about gender roles and preferences and just look at the "game."

The support of men cannot be understated. Beyond the obvious business-politik of needing male backsides in the stands as long as sports continues to

"DRAFT CAMP" BY STEPHEN BURT

We are specialists of sorts, or out of sorts. Too many people care what we are wearing.

One of us could spot a wren on a dare in a darkening glade from sixty yards away. One of us can lift any four others. One of us died. One of us stops conversations with her hawkish malachite-green eyes.

We have had repeatedly to admit that we are individual bodies, roaming through contested, crowded space, and then to believe we are part of one another, involved in very temporary combinations, minute-to-minute teams.

And why shouldn't everyone hope to be selected? Don't we all wait through life, *choose me, choose me*?

One of us can snap almost any tree limb. Another can be a tree, hard to get over, almost impossible to see around. Most of us have been called and called again.

One of us can draw blood with a glance. One can steal the sides off a scalene triangle, the green off any leaf, pickpocket the oxygen out of the air. Some of us have worked and traveled past the point of diminishing returns.

carry the perception of being a male-dominated arena, having males enjoy the women's game is a vindication for the hard efforts women ballers have, and continue, to make to improving the game.

"So many times I've gotten stopped by men and told 'you got a mad game' and that shows the support," says Minnesota Lynx star guard Seimone Augustus. "For so many years men have dominated and their support shows we're getting in there, changing things."

But the truth is that to this day—despite the Title IX, growing popularity

One and only one will be remembered in 25 years, her numbers hoisted up like constellations, winched and fixed into an outdoor sky.

And why shouldn't everyone hope to be selected? Don't we all wait through life, *choose me, choose me?*

About the author: Stephen (Steve) Burt is a dedicated fan of the WNBA—especially the Minnesota Lynx and Connecticut Sun—who lives and works as a professor of literature in St. Paul, Minnesota. Burt has penned two tomes of poetry, Shot Clocks *(Harry Tankoos Books, 2006) about the WNBA and* Parallel Play *(Graywolf, 2006). Burt can be found blogging about his love of hoops, his family, and the WNBA on Women's Hoops Blog (see chapter 12 for details).*

and recognition, and the world-class play of women from Babe Didrikson Zaharias to Billie Jean King to Mia Hamm, most of the world's sports superstars are still men. And while female presence at the average National Football League, Major League Soccer, or Major League Baseball game is growing to approach half the fans in the stands,* and women's spending on sports and sports-related merchandise is rising, the major sponsorships, glory, and fame tend to gloss over the women's efforts. Some will argue that is because the women's games just aren't as exciting to behold, their technical prowess and physical presence just not as spectacular; and to many sports fans that may be the case, but there is little doubt that women have staked out a space for themselves in the sports arena.

The more men who can appreciate the games the women put forward, the broader the appeal of the women's professional sports endeavors, and better the chance the WNBA will be here to stay.

---

*Street & Smith's SportsBusiness Journal, Dec. 24, 2001.

NINE

At the Top of Their Games

From the moment of their draft selection to the day they hang up their uniforms, players pour their heart, blood, sweat, and tears into every season, and the results since the WNBA's inception have been spectacular. From the Houston Comets' selection of Tina Thompson as the number-one draft pick on April 28, 1997, in the inaugural WNBA draft and Lisa Leslie's first slam dunk in WNBA history on July 30, 2002, to the Houston Comets four back-to-back WNBA Championships and Teresa Weatherspoon's half-court, miracle-last-seconds shot to force a third game in the 1999 WNBA finals, the WNBA's first decade was full of record-setting moments.

Hundreds of players, coaches, and support staff work diligently every year to ensure fans are treated to the finest the sport has to offer. And while each year there can be only one championship team, one most valuable player, and one defensive player of the year, the following tables are intended to pay tribute to some of the league's most valuable assets and record holders.

There are several places on the Web where fans looking for more statistical information can find various combinations of numbers, including fan forums (see chapter 12 for more details) where statistics discussions and numbers abound. One of the most central places to find a host of statistical data is at the league's Web site, WNBA.com, where, with a few clicks of the mouse, users can pull up tables based on criteria they select.

ROOKIES

Each year dozens of players join the league, selected from hundreds of hopefuls in the WNBA's spring draft, to inject young blood into the ranks of WNBA teams. Selected based on their university performance records, playing potential, and/or performance in other countries' leagues, rookies from years gone by have gone on to become some of the WNBA's most decorated players. At the end of each season, one first-year player is chosen as Rookie of the Year through a vote from a panel of sportswriters and broadcasters as having the best overall performance.

Many of the young players found on these lists have gone on to become

Number One Draft Picks

Year	Player
1997	Dena Head
1998	Margo Dydek
1999	Chamique Holdsclaw
2000	Ann Wauters
2001	Lauren Jackson
2002	Sue Bird
2003	LaToya Thomas
2004	Diana Taurasi
2005	Janel McCarville
2006	Seimone Augustus
2007	Lindsey Harding

league legends as they and their peers have added additional depth and talent to the league with every successive year.

The Number One Draft Picks list pays homage to the international character of the league and the type of talent it can draw from around the globe. Poland's Margo Dydek, Belgium's Ann Wauters, and Australia's Lauren Jackson, for example, are giants of the WNBA—figuratively *and* literally as all three are well above six feet tall! Others, like Diana Taurasi and Seimone Augustus, as relatively new as they are, are already stars in the league they love—making their marks early on the all-time leader boards.

Similarly, those players selected as Rookie of the Year have gone on to have some of the WNBA's most closely watched and decorated careers. Cheryl Ford, for example, is the only player in the league through 2007 to win Rookie of the Year honors and the WNBA Championship in the same year. Betty Lennox went on to become a WNBA Championship Most Valuable Player; Tamika Catchings has already been named Defensive Player of the Year twice.

Rookie of the Year

Year	Player	Team
1997	no award given	
1998	Tracy Reid	Charlotte
1999	Chamique Holdsclaw	Washington
2000	Betty Lennox	Minnesota
2001	Jackie Stiles	Portland
2002	Tamika Catchings	Indiana
2003	Cheryl Ford	Detroit
2004	Diana Taurasi	Phoenix
2005	Temeka Johnson	Washington
2006	Seimone Augustus	Minnesota
2007	Armintie Price	Chicago

YEARLY ACHIEVEMENTS

Each year teams, players, and coaches are awarded the league's highest honors for their efforts both on the court and off. For teams the ultimate reward is, it almost goes without saying, the WNBA Championship. The championship was originally awarded based on the results of one game, but the WNBA approved a format change in 1998 to the best of three games, after the addition of two more teams and a league-wide realignment into divisions. In 2005, the championship underwent its most recent change to a best-of-five series. No single team has made a mark on the league championship like that of the Houston Comets. Their unparalleled four straight wins established the league's first dynasty—a feat no other team has yet to match. Perhaps unsurprisingly, Houston Comets Coach Van Chancellor leads the Coach of the Year list with three straight wins.

Players and coaches are recognized for individual season achievements through votes by a panel of sportswriters and broadcasters. The champion-

WNBA Champions

Year	Winning Team	Format/Result	Opponent
1997	Houston	1 game (1-0)	New York
1998	Houston	3 games (2-1)	Phoenix
1999	Houston	3 games (2-1)	New York
2000	Houston	3 games (2-0)	New York
2001	Los Angeles	3 games (2-0)	Charlotte
2002	Los Angeles	3 games (2-0)	New York
2003	Detroit	3 games (2-1)	Los Angeles
2004	Seattle	3 games (2-1)	Connecticut
2005	Sacramento	5 games (3-1)	Connecticut
2006	Detroit	5 games (3-2)	Sacramento
2007	Phoenix	5 games (3-2)	Detroit

ship and season most-valuable-player lists read like a who's who of WNBA legends, including multiple appearances by Cynthia Cooper, Lisa Leslie, Sheryl Swoopes, and Yolanda Griffith.

The WNBA also gives out the Kim Perrot Sportsmanship Award to the player demonstrating the best sportsmanship in the league. Originally known as the WNBA Sportsmanship Award, the name was changed in honor of Houston Comets guard Kim Perrot after her 1999 death. Two-time award winner Dawn Staley, with a reputation as the quintessential professional, devoted countless hours to helping underprivileged children in her hometown of Philadelphia and cities where she played. The 2007 winner Australian Tully Bevilaqua was cited by the league for her leadership ability, knack for inspiring those around her, and her involvement in supporting cancer research, animals, and the armed forces.

WNBA Championship Most Valuable Player

Year	Player	Team
1997	Cynthia Cooper	Houston
1998	Cynthia Cooper	Houston
1999	Cynthia Cooper	Houston
2000	Cynthia Cooper	Houston
2001	Lisa Leslie	Los Angeles Sparks
2002	Lisa Leslie	Los Angeles Sparks
2003	Ruth Riley	Detroit
2004	Betty Lennox	Seattle
2005	Yolanda Griffith	Sacramento
2006	Deanna Nolan	Detroit
2007	Cappie Pondexter	Phoenix

WNBA Most Valuable Player

Year	Player	Team
1997	Cynthia Cooper	Houston
1998	Cynthia Cooper	Houston
1999	Yolanda Griffith	Sacramento
2000	Sheryl Swoopes	Houston
2001	Lisa Leslie	Los Angeles
2002	Sheryl Swoopes	Houston
2003	Lauren Jackson	Seattle
2004	Lisa Leslie	Los Angeles
2005	Sheryl Swoopes	Houston
2006	Lisa Leslie	Los Angeles
2007	Lauren Jackson	Seattle Storm

Coach of the Year

Year	Coach	Team
1997	Van Chancellor	Houston
1998	Van Chancellor	Houston
1999	Van Chancellor	Houston
2000	Michael Cooper	Los Angeles
2001	Dan Hughes	Cleveland
2002	Marianne Stanley	Washington
2003	Bill Laimbeer	Detroit
2004	Suzie McConell Serio	Minnesota
2005	John Whisenant	Sacramento
2006	Mike Thibault	Connecticut
2007	Dan Hughes	San Antonio

Defensive Player of the Year

Year	Player	Team
1997	Teresa Witherspoon	New York
1998	Teresa Witherspoon	New York
1999	Yolanda Griffith	Sacramento
2000	Sheryl Swoopes	Houston
2001	Debbie Black	Miami
2002	Sheryl Swoopes	Houston
2003	Sheryl Swoopes	Houston
2004	Lisa Leslie	Los Angeles
2005	Tamika Catchings	Indiana
2006	Tamika Catchings	Indiana
2007	Lauren Jackson	Seattle Storm

Kim Perrot Sportsmanship Award

Year	Player	Team
1997	Haixia Zheng	Los Angeles
1998	Suzie McConnell Serio	Cleveland
1999	Dawn Staley	Charlotte
2000	Suzie McConnell Serio	Cleveland
2001	Sue Wicks	New York
2002	Jennifer Gillom	Phoenix
2003	Edna Campbell	Sacramento
2004	Teresa Edwards	Minnesota
2005	Taj McWilliams-Franklin	Connecticut
2006	Dawn Staley	Houston
2007	Tully Bevilaqua	Indiana

ALL-TIME LEADERS

The following tables provide a record of individual achievements in a sampling of the most commonly tracked categories as of September 2007. For fans of the league, there's hardly a player on these lists who is not a household name with a hardcore group of fans who loves her. Some like Lisa Leslie, Sheryl Swoopes, and Tina Thompson have been racking up points, steals, and rebounds since the league began and are perceived as nearing the end of their WNBA days. Others like Seimone Augustus, Katie Douglas, Lauren Jackson, and Diana Taurasi have time to increase their totals and attempt to push the other leaders, including retired legends like Cynthia Cooper and Teresa Weatherspoon, down in the rankings.

Total Points

Rank	Player	Points
1	Lisa Leslie	5,412
2	Tina Thompson	4,882
3	Katie Smith	4,577
4	Sheryl Swoopes	4,399
5	Lauren Jackson	4,177
6	Yolanda Griffith	4,002
7	Chamique Holdsclaw	3,975
8	Nykesha Sales	3,955
9	Tangela Smith	3,846
10	Vickie Johnson	3,826

Points per Game

Rank	Player	Games	FGs	FTs	Points	Points per Game
1	Seimone Augustus	68	579	299	1,513	22.3
2	Cynthia Cooper	124	802	758	2,601	21.0
3	Diana Taurasi	133	888	468	2,578	19.4
4	Lauren Jackson	216	1,466	960	4,177	19.3
5	Cappie Pondexter	63	412	249	1,156	18.3
6	Chamique Holdsclaw	225	1,531	855	3,975	17.7
7	Lisa Leslie	307	2,000	1,295	5,412	17.6
8	Tamika Catchings	187	1,012	883	3,203	17.1
9	Sheryl Swoopes	262	1,652	868	4,399	16.8
10	Alana Beard	129	770	427	2,104	16.3

Three Pointers/Field Goals Made

Rank	Player	FG Attempted	FG Percentage	FG Made
1	Katie Smith	1,651	.362	598
2	Tina Thompson	1,192	.368	439
3	Crystal Robinson	1,138	.374	426
4	Becky Hammon	1,092	.371	405
5	Mwadi Mabika	1,209	.329	398
6	Nykesha Sales	990	.356	352
7	Allison Feaster	1,007	.347	349
8	Diana Taurasi	931	.359	334
9	Katie Douglas	896	.356	319
10	Sue Bird	817	.387	316

Free Throws Made

Rank	Player	FT Attempts	FT Percentage	FT Made
1	Lisa Leslie	1,858	.697	1,295
2	Katie Smith	1,332	.858	1,143
3	Yolanda Griffith	1,591	.718	1,142
4	Tina Thompson	1,209	.818	989
5	Lauren Jackson	1,158	.829	960
6	Shannon Johnson	1,194	.760	908
7	Tamika Catchings	1,075	.821	883
8	Sheryl Swoopes	1,046	.830	868
9	Chamique Holdsclaw	1,083	.789	855
10	Chasity Melvin	1,157	.694	803

Total Steals

Rank	Player	Games	Steals per Game	Steals
1	Sheryl Swoopes	262	2.25	589
2	Ticha Penichiero	306	1.92	588
3	Nykesha Sales	278	1.76	490
4	Yolanda Griffith	278	1.75	486
5	Tamika Catchings	187	2.58	483
6	Teresa Weatherspoon	254	1.83	465
7	Lisa Leslie	307	1.39	427
8	Sheri Sam	296	1.42	419
9	Shannon Johnson	285	1.46	415
10	DeLisha Milton-Jones	268	1.51	406

Total Rebounds

Rank	Player	Games	Off.	Def.	Rebounds Per Game	Rebounds
1	Lisa Leslie	307	742	2,121	9.3	2,863
2	Yolanda Griffith	278	968	1,280	8.1	2,248
3	Margo Dydek	321	363	1,777	6.7	2,140
4	Tina Thompson	302	614	1,389	6.6	2,003
5	Taj McWilliams-Franklin	272	718	1,266	7.3	1,984
6	Chamique Holdsclaw	225	532	1,330	8.3	1,862
7	Natalie Williams	221	733	1,099	8.3	1,832
8	Wendy Palmer	311	534	1,291	5.9	1,825
9	Lauren Jackson	216	515	1,225	8.1	1,740
10	Tangela Smith	322	510	1,170	5.2	1,680

Total Blocks

Rank	Player	Games	Average	Blocks
1	Margo Dydek	321	2.73	877
2	Lisa Leslie	307	2.25	692
3	Lauren Jackson	216	2.09	452
4	Tangela Smith	322	1.31	423
5	Ruth Riley	223	1.58	352
6	Tammy Sutton-Brown	227	1.48	335
7	Elena Baranova	209	1.53	320
8	Yolanda Griffith	278	1.09	304
9	Taj McWilliams-Franklin	272	1.09	297
10	Vicky Bullett	186	1.55	288

TEN

The Best of the Best: Fan Favorites

S etting out to pick a selection of the WNBA's greatest players as examples for newer fans of the league seemed an easy proposition before actually sitting down to compile a representative list. Each player has brought with her years of practice and play devoted to the game she loves. Many displayed inspiring levels of guts, determination, and sheer heart to overcome physical limitations, injuries, personal loses, or socio-economic limitations (to name just a few of the many challenges along the way) on their rise to the upper echelons of women's basketball. Each has brought her own particular talents, personality, quirks, and elements of that special "x" factor that will forever imprint the images of her WNBA years in fans' memories.

In the end it seemed that the best—if not the most scientific—way to find that elusive list of women who most exemplify the best the WNBA has to offer was to ask the thousands of fans who plan their entire summers around league games: the devoted cadre of women's hoops aficionados who rant and rage when unable to access a game either on television, radio, or the Internet, that passionate group of people from around the world to whom legends of the WNBA will ever be heroines who trail blazed a new era of women's basketball in the United States.

So in June and July of 2007, the call went out to WNBA fans across the globe to vote for their all-time favorite WNBA players based on "skill, longevity, personality, or just because a player made you love the game—in other words your favorites!" Several fan forums, Web sites, blogs, and boards, including Rebkell's Junkie Boards, She's Got Game, Women's Hoops Blog, the Minnesota Women's Basketball Forum, and Women's Basketball Online, took up the challenge and got the word out, urged their communities to vote, and helped ensure this author had more than her own votes to count when it came time to add up the final tally.

The results? Amazing. Hundreds of fans cast thousands of votes. Some fans chafed at being asked to limit their list to a top ten; others went ahead and listed all their favorites regardless of the ten-player limit. A few heated online arguments ensued over peoples' choices. Several rounds of eye-crossing counts of lists were completed.

And when the dust settled, we ended up with the following list of the top ten all-time fan favorites. Some of the players who made the list can still be seen on the WNBA courts; some have moved on to coach in the WNBA and elsewhere; others can be found commenting from the sidelines on the game they still love. But wherever these women are now, their contributions are invaluable to the game and highlight the WNBA's best—past, present, and future.

In an author's recognition that selecting just ten is an extremely difficult process, you'll also find a nod to those who ended up in slots 11–15 in the vote results (though you'll notice a few players tied for that last spot). Again, this list could have gone on for several chapters, and while the women profiled herein are phenomenal, they are by no means the only great players ever to step out onto the court.

Any statistical data and team affiliations go through the 2007 season for active players unless otherwise indicated; last season played for retired or deceased players.

Statistics Key

OR	Offensive Rebound
STG	Steals per Game
DR	Defensive Rebound
BPG	Blocks per Game
RPG	Rebounds per Game
PPG	Points per Game
APG	Assists per Game

1. TAMIKA CATCHINGS ("CATCH" OR "MIKA")

Indian Fever
#24, Forward
July 21, 1979

Catchings's dazzling on-court presence (and absolutely bruising play against anyone trying to keep the ball out of her hands) can, at first, seem at odds with the stout heart and warm smile she has for the fans. But her determination on the court is actually a profound reflection of who she is off the court—a determined campaigner for change who participates not only in many community outreach programs but runs her own foundation, Catch the Stars (see chapter 11 for more on this).

Catchings played her college ball at the University of Tennessee from

1997–2001 under legendary coach Pat Summitt, where she led the team in scoring (15.1 points per game) and rebounding (8.6 per game) and graduated with a degree in sports management. During her Tennessee tenure she was named a Kodak All-American four seasons in a row. By the time Catchings earned her master's degree four years later in May 2005, the Stratford, New Jersey, native was an established international women's basketball star.

The Fever drafted Catchings in the first round (third overall) ahead of the 2001 season and she would go on to take Rookie of the Year honors in 2002. Her basketball resume is filled with All-Star Game appearances (including 2002, 2003, and 2007) and Defensive Player of the Year awards in 2005 and 2006, as well as three gold medals, a silver, and a bronze medal as a member of the USA Women's Senior Basketball Team—most notably a 2002 FIBA World Championships for Women gold and a 2004 Olympic gold medal. Catchings also played with the National Women's Basketball League's Chicago Blaze for parts of two seasons between 2003 and 2005, and overseas in South Korea.

Catchings's family is never far from her side. Her sister, Tauja, also a talented basketball player in her own right and color analyst for the Chicago Sky, is the vice president of the Catch the Stars Foundation and is seen often at WNBA games with her young son and the head of the Catchings clan, her father, Harvey. Catchings wears number 24 in honor of her family, all of whom she considers her role models and greatest source of inspiration. Her father, an eleven-year veteran of the NBA, wore 42 (the reverse of 24), her brother Kenyon wore 21 (half of 42), and her sister wore 12 (half of 24).

Catchings has had her share of challenges and disappointments to overcome. Born with severe hearing loss in both ears and forced to wear hearing aids as child, Catchings poured her heart and soul into basketball (under the tutelage of her father) as a way to overcome. While she left the University of Tennessee a bona fide star-in-the-making, Catchings had sat out part of the last season with an anterior cruciate ligament tear that would also keep her benched for her first professional season. The end of the 2007 season also brought disappointment as Catchings, who missed the end of the regular season with a partial tear of the plantar fascia in the left foot, went down in the decisive third game of the postseason's Eastern Conference Championship game just before the end of the first half, with what would later be determined to be an Achilles tendon injury to her right ankle.

Not yet thirty years old, Catchings is likely to remain a fixture in the WNBA for several years to come. And if her dogged sense of determination (which saw Catchings attempt to go back on court for the second half of that 2006 Eastern Conference game, with a torn Achilles that would later require surgery) continues to carry her forward, she's unlikely to quit before she can add WNBA Champion to her resume.

CAREER SEASON AVERAGES FOR TAMIKA CATCHINGS

Year	OR	DR	RPG	APG	SPG	BPG	PPG
2002	2.9	5.8	8.6	3.7	2.9	1.3	18.6
2003	2.4	5.6	8.0	3.4	2.1	1.0	19.7
2004	2.3	5.0	7.3	3.4	2.0	1.1	16.7
2005	2.0	5.7	7.8	4.2	2.7	0.5	14.7
2006	2.1	5.4	7.5	3.7	2.9	1.1	16.3
2007	2.6	6.4	9.0	4.7	3.1	1.0	16.6

CAREER TOTALS (THROUGH 2007) FOR TAMIKA CATCHINGS

Games	OR	DR	Rebounds	Assists	Steals	Blocks	Points
187	444	1,046	1,490	707	483	189	3,203

2. DIANA TAURASI ("DT" OR "DEE")

Phoenix Mercury
#3, Guard
June 11, 1982

In women's hoops circles, this bold, brassy, and sassy Chino, California, native became a household name even before she hit the WNBA. Taurasi is dynamite on the court, fiercely competitive, and full of attitude. Off the court, her fierceness translates into a wicked sense of humor, sarcasm, and a big, broad grin she playfully flashes after lobbing various sports-related paraphernalia (Ace bandages, socks, towels, and anything else she can reach) at teammates across a locker room.

Diana Taurasi

Taurasi excelled during her years of play at the University of Connecticut, averaging fifteen points, 4.3 rebounds, and 4.5 assists per game, and helped lead the Huskies to three straight NCAA Championships. Along the way the sociology major was twice named a Kodak All-American, the 2003 Wade Trophy winner, and the 2003–2004 NCAA Basketball Tournament's Most Outstanding Player.

At the international level, Taurasi earned her chops early as a member of the 2001 USA Junior World Championship winning team. Three years later,

CAREER SEASON AVERAGES FOR DIANA TAURASI

Year	OR	DR	RPG	APG	SPG	BPG	PPG
2004	0.8	3.6	4.4	3.9	1.3	0.7	17.0
2005	0.7	3.5	4.2	4.5	1.1	0.9	16.0
2006	0.7	2.9	3.6	4.1	1.2	0.8	25.3
2007	0.6	3.7	4.2	4.3	1.4	1.1	19.2

CAREER TOTALS (THROUGH 2007) FOR DIANA TAURASI

Games	OR	DR	Rebounds	Assists	Steals	Blocks	Points
133	93	451	544	558	168	114	2,578

she would help propel the USA women's team to Olympic gold in Athens and follow that with a 2006 bronze medal win at the World Championships in Brazil, before turning her sights on the 2008 Beijing Olympics.

The Mercury snapped up Taurasi as the first overall draft pick in 2004, and watched with glee as the new pro averaged seventeen points and 4.4 rebounds per game that season on her way to being named 2004 Rookie of the Year. Taurasi's bold style and consistent results helped earn her three back-to-back All-Star appearances in 2005, 2006, and 2007.

Still early into her professional career, Taurasi has already joined the elite group of female athletes (which includes Sheryl Swoopes, Dawn Staley, Sue Bird, and Lisa Leslie) to have a Nike shoe named after her—the DT Shox.

Despite her tough on-court presence, Taurasi has a softer side, especially when it comes to kids to whom she donates time and effort through her Diana Taurasi Foundation (see chapter 11 for more details).

Taurasi made her debut WNBA finals appearance in 2007, helping the Mercury clinch a nail-biting win over reigning champions Detroit Shock. With the Mercury's 2007 championship win, Taurasi joins an elite club of players who have won the U.S. women's basketball triple—NCAA Championship, WNBA Championship, and Olympic gold. Not yet thirty, the feisty Taurasi has plenty of game yet to play and will be looking to add even more accolades to her already impressive resume.

3. LAUREN JACKSON ("LOJACK" "LOZ" OR "LJ")

Seattle Storm
#15, Forward-Center
May 11, 1981

Jackson is one of the world's most well-known female basketballers, with a huge following not only in her home country of Australia but also in the United States, Asia, and Europe. Her on-court domination is an imposing combination of long legs that can outstrip, outjump, and just plain exhaust most of her fellow ballers, as well as blocking and scoring prowess that make the Aussie a triple threat all on her own.

This Australian was born with basketball in her blood and was barely out of diapers when she began playing in earnest at age four. Her parents, Gary and Maree Jackson, had both played hoops, both with Australia's national teams (Gary in 1975, Maree from 1974 to 1982). Jackson wears her mother's number—15—in her honor.

She quickly went on to become a basketball prodigy at Murray High School in her hometown of Albury, before moving on to the Australian Institute of Sport in Canberra. In 1997, Jackson became the youngest player, then only sixteen, ever selected to play for Australia's national team, the Opals. Jackson has appeared more than sixty times internationally with the Opals, including back-to-back silver medal runs at the 2000 Sydney and 2004 Athens Olympics, and a bronze medal at the 1998 World Championships. After her

Juliette Terzieff

Storm star Lauren Jackson at the 2007 All-Star game

sport institute days, Jackson continued to play in Canberra for the Capitals, leading them to four back-to-back titles.

Jackson joined the WNBA when the Seattle Storm grabbed her as first overall pick in the 2001 draft. Her dominating presence was felt immediately as the six-foot-five Aussie terrorized defenses with her forceful rebounding and scoring capabilities. By 2003, the young Jackson, then only twenty-four, was already a budding WNBA legend—and was recognized as such when she became the first international player to be named WNBA Most Valuable

CAREER SEASON AVERAGES FOR LAUREN JACKSON

Year	OR	DR	RPG	APG	SPG	BPG	PPG
2001	2.0	4.7	6.7	1.5	1.9	2.2	15.2
2002	2.4	4.4	6.8	1.5	1.1	2.9	17.2
2003	2.5	6.8	9.3	1.9	1.1	1.9	21.2
2004	2.1	4.6	6.7	1.6	1.0	2.0	20.5
2005	2.8	6.4	9.2	1.7	1.1	2.0	17.6
2006	2.3	5.3	7.6	1.6	0.8	1.7	19.5
2007	2.6	7.1	9.6	1.3	1.0	2.0	23.8

CAREER TOTALS (THROUGH 2007) FOR LAUREN JACKSON

Games	OR	DR	Rebounds	Assists	Steals	Blocks	Points
216	515	1,225	1,740	343	244	452	4,177

Player. The following year, the Storm would block out the Connecticut Sun for the team's first WNBA Championship. In 2007, Jackson's dominant force on the court would propel the Aussie to a second WNBA Most Valuable Player award.

Jackson is already a feature of the league's all-time leader statistics records (see chapter 9), ranking in the top ten for total points scored, blocks, free throws made, and points per game. Although she's indicated she will leave the WNBA if the Storm relocate away from Seattle, with many years of professional playing time ahead of her the already impressive resume of this surprisingly soft spoken and humble Aussie is equally likely to see additional accolades added in the years to come.

4. SHERYL SWOOPES ("HER MAJESTY")

Houston Comets
#22, Forward
March 25, 1971

The undisputed queen of U.S. women's basketball, Swoopes has repeatedly been called the "female Michael Jordan." There is hardly a benchmark she hasn't achieved, and quite a few for which the Brownfield, Texas, native set the standard of greatness.

Swoopes began her college career at South Plains Junior College but transferred over to Texas Tech, where she led the Lady Raiders to the 1993 NCAA Championship with 177 points in four games. During her Texas Tech years, Swoopes recreated the NCAA record books in five categories—records that continued to stand as late as 2006.

Among her many WNBA milestones, Swoopes began her march toward legendary status early on as part of the Houston Comets dynasty triple-threat offense (alongside Cynthia Cooper and Tina Thompson) that would propel the team to an unrivaled four back-to-back WNBA Championships.

Swoopes recorded the WNBA's first triple-double (fifteen points, fourteen rebounds and ten assists) on July 27, 1999, during a Comets win over the Shock, made six WNBA All-Star appearances, was the first female athlete assigned a Nike shoe—the "Air Swoopes"—and is one of only two WNBA players to have three Olympic gold medals in her war chest (Lisa Leslie is the other). Swoopes and Leslie featured on the USA women's basketball squads

CAREER SEASON AVERAGES FOR SHERYL SWOOPES

Year	OR	DR	RPG	APG	SPG	BPG	PPG
1997	0.7	1.0	1.7	0.8	0.8	0.4	7.1
1998	1.3	3.8	5.1	2.1	2.5	0.5	15.6
1999	1.5	4.8	6.3	4.0	2.4	1.4	18.3
2000	1.3	5.0	6.3	3.8	2.8	1.1	20.7
2002	0.9	4.0	4.9	3.3	2.8	0.7	18.5
2003	1.0	3.6	4.6	3.9	2.5	0.8	15.6
2004	1.2	3.7	4.9	2.9	1.5	0.5	14.8
2005	0.8	2.8	3.6	4.3	2.0	0.8	18.6
2006	1.1	4.8	5.9	2.7	2.1	0.3	15.5
2007	1.0	4.7	5.7	2.7	1.7	0.3	7.7

CAREER TOTALS (THROUGH 2007) FOR SHERYL SWOOPES

Games	OR	DR	Rebounds	Assists	Steals	Blocks	Points
262	297	1,037	1,334	901	589	198	4,399

that won in Atlanta (1996), Sydney (2000), and Athens (2004). Swoopes has also been honored three times as the WNBA Most Valuable Player (2000, 2002, and 2005) and three times as the league's Defensive Player of the Year in 2000, 2002, and 2003.

Over the years Swoopes experienced life's personal ups and downs under the glaring spotlight of being a public figure. She sat out much of the 1997 season to give birth to her son, Jordan Eric, battled through the press of her 1999 divorce from her high school sweetheart, and bravely stepped forward in 2005 to announce that she was in love with a woman and tired of hiding a relationship so central to her happiness. Swoopes's declaration hardly caused a ripple among the legions of fans who continue to embrace the star and proved, yet again, that persistent homophobia serves only to damage people who have phenomenal contributions to make to the world around them.

With a back injury that left Swoopes sidelined for the 2007 WNBA season, many fans believed this legend's days on the court had ended, leaving her free to pursue the sports broadcasting career she had repeatedly indicated to be her next move.

5. CYNTHIA COOPER ("COOP")

Houston Comets
#14, Guard
April 14, 1963

By the time the WNBA came into existence, Cooper had already spent a decade playing professionally in Europe and had medaled in two consecutive Olympic Games. The Los Angeles, California, native returned home to become a member of the Houston Comets legendary triple-threat offense (along side Sheryl Swoopes and Tina Thompson) that set the league alight with four straight WNBA Championship wins.

Cooper's basketball glory began with 1983 and 1984 NCAA Championship wins with the USC Lady Trojans. With no opportunities at home, Cooper debuted professionally in Europe, playing eleven years, including seasons in Segovia, Spain (1987); Parma, Italy (1988 through 1994, and 1997); and Alcamo, Italy (1995 and 1996). The feisty five-foot-ten guard traveled to Seoul, Korea, in 1988 to help the USA women's national team bring home a gold medal and returned four years later to capture a bronze medal at the 1992 Olympics in Barcelona, Spain.

In 1995, Cooper worked briefly as an assistant coach at the University of Houston before her love of the game drove her back to Italy.

When the opportunity came to return home to play in front of family and

CAREER SEASON AVERAGES FOR CYNTHIA COOPER

Year	OR	DR	RPG	APG	SPG	BPG	PPG
1997	1.2	2.8	4.0	4.7	2.1	0.21	22.2
1998	0.8	2.8	3.6	4.4	1.6	0.37	22.7
1999	0.5	2.3	2.8	5.2	1.39	0.35	22.1
2000	0.5	2.2	2.7	5.0	1.26	0.19	17.7
2003	0.5	2.0	2.5	5.5	1.00	0.25	16.0

CAREER TOTALS (THROUGH 2003) FOR CYNTHIA COOPER

Games	OR	DR	Rebounds	Assists	Steals	Blocks	Points
124	94	309	403	602	193	35	2,601

friends, Cooper did so gloriously, earning the WNBA's first—and second—Most Valuable Player awards in 1997 and 1998, as an integral part of the core group of players who helped Houston emerge as the league's first bona fide dynasty. Cooper was also the first player to reach 500, 1,000, 2,000, and 2,500 points in the WNBA.

While everyone in the WNBA and all the fans were stunned and saddened by the passing of Kim Perrot in 1999, Cooper was absolutely devastated by the loss. In her 1999 autobiography, *She Got Game,,* Cooper called the experience of watching her own mother, Mary Cobb, and one of the closest friends she'd ever had, Perrot, both succumb to cancer in the same year as one of the hardest periods of her life.

She left the courts for a spot on the sidelines as coach of the Phoenix Mercury for the 2001 and 2002 seasons, before returning to the Comets roster in 2003. The return was ultimately limited to four games as a torn rotator cuff forced the basketball great to hang up her professional jersey for good at age forty-one.

Cooper, actually now Cooper-Dyke, is head coach at Prairie View A&M and was named as assistant coach for the USA Women's Under 19 National Team in March 2007. She is also a mother of twins with husband Brian Dyke.

6. KATIE SMITH

Detroit Shock
#30, Guard
June 4, 1974

Lurking behind Smith's playful smile is a fierce trio of innate talents—speed, agility, and accuracy—that have helped make the Ohio native the first woman in American women's professional basketball history to score five thousand points (in 2005), and the only one so far to score six thousand (in

2007) career points (achieved through her play in the ABL and WNBA). As if that wasn't enough, Smith is also a prolific defender who routinely frustrates even the most talented offensive players.

Her record setting began early, as Smith left Ohio State with a zoology degree and a place in the history books—as the leading scorer in Big Ten women's basketball history with 2,598 points. Her collegiate record would

CAREER SEASON AVERAGES FOR KATIE SMITH

Year	OR	DR	RPG	APG	SPG	BPG	PPG
1999	1.4	1.5	2.9	2.0	0.6	0.3	11.7
2000	0.9	2.0	2.9	2.8	1.4	0.2	20.2
2001	1.3	2.6	3.9	2.2	0.7	0.2	23.1
2002	0.8	2.2	3.0	2.5	1.0	0.2	16.5
2003	1.2	2.9	4.1	2.5	0.7	0.2	18.2
2004	0.7	2.9	3.7	2.3	1.0	0.3	18.8
2005(MIN)	0.5	1.9	2.4	2.7	1.1	0.1	13.3
2005(DET)	0.8	1.3	2.2	2.0	0.4	0.2	9.5
2006	0.6	2.1	2.7	3.3	0.7	0.1	11.7
2007	0.5	3.2	3.8	3.6	1.2	0.1	13.2

CAREER TOTALS (THROUGH 2007) FOR KATIE SMITH

Games	OR	DR	Rebounds	Assists	Steals	Blocks	Points
286	251	669	920	758	263	53	4,577

fall to Penn State's Kelly Mazzante in 2004, but by then Smith was already on track to set records in the pro leagues.

Smith launched her professional career in 1996 with the ABL's Columbus Quest, winning two championships before the league folded in 1999. For six years she applied her skills to the efforts of the Minnesota Lynx, before being traded to the Detroit Shock ahead of the team's 2006 Championship-winning season. The win made Smith the only player to have won championships in both the ABL and WNBA.

Smith also boasts two Olympic gold medals (2000 and 2004) as well as two World Championship gold medals (1998 and 2002), and a World Championship bronze in 2006. She has also been selected six times as a WNBA All-Star (2000, 2001, 2002, 2003, 2005, and 2006).

By the end of the 2007 season there wasn't much in women's basketball Smith had not already done and/or won, but Smith's legendary competitive nature made it a pretty sure bet the world-class guard still had more hoops left to play. When the time comes to shed the basketball uniform Smith, who has been attending dental school in the off season, plans to shift strategy and focus on plaque offensive.

7. TERESA WEATHERSPOON ("T-SPOON" OR "SPOON")

Los Angeles Sparks
#11, Guard
December 8, 1965

Weatherspoon's passion and natural charisma helped the Pineland, Texas, native win over the hearts of fans in the Big Apple the same way she emerged as the New York Liberty's inspirational leader. The team charged out of the WNBA starting blocks winning the league's first-ever game and secured a trip to the league's inaugural Championship game. While the Liberty would end up "always the bride's maid, never the bride" in four attempts at the WNBA Championship in five years (1997, 1999, 2000, and 2001), Weatherspoon is widely regarded amongst women's hoops fans as one of the most positive forces in the WNBA's first decade.

Weatherspoon played her collegiate ball at Louisiana Tech, helping bring home a 1988 NCAA Championship in her senior year. Later that summer, Weatherspoon would help give USA women's basketball a gold medal–

CAREER SEASON AVERAGES FOR TERESA WEATHERSPOON

Year	OR	DR	RPG	APG	SPG	BPG	PPG
1997	0.9	3.3	4.1	6.1	3.04	0.07	7.0
1998	0.7	3.3	4.0	6.4	3.33	0.00	6.8
1999	0.7	2.6	3.3	6.4	2.44	0.09	7.2
2000	0.5	2.9	3.4	6.4	2.03	0.16	6.4
2001	0.9	2.8	3.7	6.3	1.72	0.13	6.5
2002	0.7	2.0	2.7	5.7	1.31	0.09	3.4
2003	0.6	2.3	2.9	4.4	0.82	0.15	2.9
2004	0.2	0.7	0.9	0.9	0.35	0.03	0.5

CAREER TOTALS (THROUGH 2007) FOR TERESA WEATHERSPOON

Games	OR	DR	Rebounds	Assists	Steals	Blocks	Points
254	160	619	779	1,338	465	23	1,264

winning performance. In 1992, she returned to the Olympic podium to collect a bronze medal.

When the WNBA began to recruit players, Weatherspoon returned from Europe to join the New York Liberty. Like the team, Weatherspoon achieved immediate success, emerging as the WNBA's Defensive Player of the Year in both 1997 and 1998. She would make four WNBA All-Star appearances (1999, 2000, 2001, and 2002) and be the first player in the league to reach one thousand assists—which she did against the Shock on June 5, 2002.

WNBA fans have many cherished memories of T-Spoon, many of them centered on her engaged interaction with fans. But, for most fans, it is Weatherspoon's sixty-foot, half-court, buzzer-beating basket that took the New York Liberty to victory in the second game of the 1999 finals against the Houston Comets that best exemplifies the many contributions she made to the league. That iconic shot set the standard for league greatness and demonstrated Weatherspoon's belief in never giving up no matter what the odds. At the league's ten-year mark a fan vote to pick the WNBA's Greatest Moment awarded Weatherspoon the honor for that jaw-dropping historic play.

Weatherspoon retired in 2004, playing her last season in Los Angeles, but can still be found on the sidelines of WNBA games cheering the players on. The legendary guard, who now writes computer software, continues to feed her basketball love through youth camps and community work.

8. YOLANDA GRIFFITH ("YO" OR "YO-YO")

Sacramento Monarchs
#33, Center-Forward
March 1, 1970

Known to many of her competitors as the loose ball queen, Griffith has an almost uncanny knack for battling through the league's best ballers to come up with a rebound. With the second highest number of career rebounds in the league—2,248—Griffith's fierce pursuit of the ball helped propel the Sacramento Monarchs to the 2005 WNBA Championships and garnered Championship Most Valuable Player honors for the Chicago native.

Griffith's road to the top wasn't always smooth. Though she was offered a scholarship to play collegiate ball at the University of Iowa, Griffith turned it down, gave birth to her daughter, and headed to Florida's Palm Beach Junior

CAREER SEASON AVERAGES FOR YOLANDA GRIFFITH

Year	OR	DR	RPG	APG	SPG	BPG	PPG
1999	4.9	6.5	11.4	1.6	2.5	1.9	18.8
2000	4.6	5.7	10.3	1.5	2.6	1.9	16.3
2001	5.1	6.1	11.2	1.7	2.0	1.2	16.2
2002	3.9	4.8	8.7	1.1	0.9	0.8	16.9
2003	2.7	4.6	7.3	1.4	1.7	1.1	13.8
2004	3.6	3.6	7.2	1.2	2.2	1.2	14.5
2005	2.6	4.0	6.6	1.5	1.2	0.9	13.8
2006	2.6	3.9	6.4	1.6	1.3	0.5	12.0
2007	2.0	2.6	4.6	1.5	1.0	0.4	9.0

CAREER TOTALS (THROUGH 2007) FOR YOLANDA GRIFFITH

Games	OR	DR	Rebounds	Assists	Steals	Blocks	Points
278	968	1,280	2,248	408	486	304	4,002

College and then Florida Atlantic University. To support herself, Griffith took a job in repossessions where she learned how to jimmy a lock and hot-wire a car. After she graduated in 1993, Griffith headed to Europe to play professional basketball.

Griffith was the number-one pick, selected by the Long Beach Sting Rays, in the ABL's 1997 draft. She was traded to the Chicago Condors after one season, and later moved to the Sacramento Monarchs when the ABL folded in 1999.

From there her march into the record books turned into a sprint. Griffith was named WNBA Defensive Player of the Year and Most Valuable Player in 1999. The next year she would win Olympic gold—an accomplishment she and her USA women's basketball teammates would repeat in 2004. In 2005, after the Monarchs beat the Connecticut Sun in the finals, Griffiths was named WNBA Championships Most Valuable Player. Griffiths has made seven WNBA All-Star appearances—a feat matched by only three other players through the 2007 season: Lisa Leslie, Nykesha Sales, and Tina Thompson.

Griffiths has indicated that when she retires, she'd like to turn her attention to a different kind of court and pursue a career in law enforcement.

9. BECKY HAMMON ("BECKSTER")

San Antonio Silver Stars
#25, Guard
March 11, 1977

This self-described easygoing country girl from Rapid City, South Dakota, certainly looks more Faith Hill than Layla Ali, but put her on the court and Hammon demonstrates that she is *the* example in the WNBA of the old adage "don't judge a book by its cover." Hammon would hardly be considered short in nonbasketball situations—in fact, she's taller than the average five-foot-four height of an American woman—but at five-foot-six Hammon regularly plays against ballers with distinct height advantages.

Hammon's Colorado State collegiate career unfolded in a flurry of record-setting performances as she posted all-time records in seven categories, including total points (2,740), points per game (21.9), and assists (538). During her senior year Hammon helped lead the Rams to the NCAA Sweet Sixteen. In November 2004, Hammon was inducted into the Colorado State Univer-

CAREER SEASON AVERAGES FOR BECKY HAMMON

Year	OR	DR	RPG	APG	SPG	BPG	PPG
1999	0.1	0.6	0.7	0.6	0.2	0.0	2.7
2000	0.6	1.4	2.0	1.8	0.9	0.0	11.0
2001	0.3	1.3	1.6	1.6	0.8	0.0	8.2
2002	0.6	1.6	2.2	1.7	0.8	0.0	8.0
2003	0.1	1.8	1.9	1.6	0.9	0.1	14.7
2004	0.5	3.0	3.5	4.4	1.7	0.1	13.5
2005	0.6	2.8	3.4	4.3	1.8	0.1	13.9
2006	0.3	2.7	3.0	3.7	1.3	0.1	14.7
2007	0.3	2.5	2.8	5.0	0.8	0.2	18.8

CAREER TOTALS (THROUGH 2007) FOR BECKY HAMMON

Games	OR	DR	Rebounds	Assists	Steals	Blocks	Points
255	101	498	599	715	267	15	2,894

sity Hall of Fame. Just a few months later the university retired her jersey.

The spunky guard entered the WNBA undrafted in 1999, landing a place on the New York Liberty's star-studded roster as a backup to Teresa Weatherspoon. Within a couple of years, Hammon was the team's starting point guard and cocaptain—and a huge favorite with New York fans.

Hammon has made four appearances as a WNBA All-Star and played several seasons with the National Women's Basketball League's Tennessee Fury and Colorado Chill, helping the Chill win back-to-back titles in 2005 and 2006.

Although Hammon was stunned to learn she was on the trading block when the Liberty sent her to San Antonio in an April draft-day trade before the 2007 season, she helped lead the Stars into the postseason. Hammon left behind legions of adoring Liberty fans (and a namesake "Hammon Eggs and Cheese" sandwich at New York's Carnegie Deli restaurant) but quickly attracted new fans with her easygoing style and vicious on-court play.

Just into her thirties, Hammon is unlikely to end her playing career before she takes a few more shots at bringing home a WNBA Championship. Hammon has expressed a desire to coach at the high school or collegiate level when she does retire but has made several successful broadcast appearances in the off-season as a sideline reporter covering NBA games for ESPN.

10. TINA THOMPSON ("LIPS")

Houston Comets
#7, Forward
February 10, 1975

From her veteran leadership on the court to her eloquent expression of her love for the game off the court, Thompson is one of the WNBA's most enduring—and endearing—ambassadors. That, and she's one hell of a ball player.

CAREER SEASON AVERAGES FOR TINA THOMPSON

Year	OR	DR	RPG	APG	SPG	BPG	PPG
1997	2.4	4.2	6.6	1.1	0.8	1.0	13.2
1998	2.4	4.7	7.1	0.9	1.1	0.9	12.7
1999	2.1	4.3	6.4	0.9	1.0	1.0	12.2
2000	2.1	5.5	7.7	1.5	1.5	0.8	16.9
2001	2.8	5.0	7.8	1.9	1.0	0.7	19.3
2002	2.3	5.2	7.5	2.1	0.9	0.7	16.7
2003	1.4	4.5	5.9	1.7	0.6	0.8	16.9
2004	1.7	4.3	6.0	1.8	0.9	0.9	20.0
2005	1.1	2.7	3.8	1.5	0.8	0.3	10.1
2006	1.5	4.1	5.6	2.2	0.9	0.6	18.7
2007	1.9	4.8	6.7	2.8	0.9	0.7	18.8

CAREER TOTALS (THROUGH 2007) FOR TINA THOMPSON

Games	OR	DR	Rebounds	Assists	Steals	Blocks	Points
302	614	1,389	2,003	510	285	237	4,882

Like many of the WNBA legends, Thompson grew up playing basketball against boys, which led her to develop an outside game to compete effectively against stronger opponents. Little did those boys know Thompson was developing a game that would go on to terrorize defenses across the nation.

Thompson played her collegiate ball at USC, helping to lead the team to three NCAA tournaments (1994, 1995, and 1997) before being selected first in the WNBA's inaugural 1997 draft. Since then, she's won Olympic gold (at the 2004 Athens Games), appeared seven times as a WNBA All-Star (1999, 2000, 2001, 2002, 2003, 2006, and 2007), and reigned over the WNBA with her fellow Comets with four back-to-back WNBA Championship wins (1997–2000). She was also the league's second top scorer of all time with 4,882 points through the 2007 season and has the WNBA's second highest number of three-pointers made.

As the WNBA marked the end of its first decade, Thompson was one of only a handful of the league's original players still active on the court. Thompson surprised fans during the 2007 season when she indicated she might leave the WNBA to play out her remaining competitive years in Europe, where salaries are higher. With a young son, Dylan, to take care of, many fans expressed sympathy with her thinking. When she finally chooses to hang up her uniform for the final time Thompson, who already has a degree in sociology, has indicated a desire to pursue a law degree.

11. DEANNA NOLAN ("TWEETY")

Detroit Shock

#14, Guard-Forward

August 25, 1979

Nolan spent her college years with the University of Georgia Lady Bull-dogs—averaging a career eleven points, 2.9 assists, and 4.5 rebounds per game—as they headed to the 1999 NCAA Final Four and the 2000 NCAA Elite Eight.

Nolan launched her professional career in 2001, drafted in the first round by the Detroit Shock, and immediately began what would be a long-distance run into the record books. From her rookie season through 2007, the Flint, Michigan, native consistently placed at the top of the free throw percentage, three pointers made, assists, and steals leader boards for the league. Nolan, who primarily plays the point guard position but is also an adept shooting guard, has maintained a point-per-game average in double figures since 2003, helping lead her team to two WNBA Championships, in 2003 and 2006. In 2006, Nolan was named the championship series' Most Valuable Player.

Nolan joined her teammates Swin Cash, Cheryl Ford, and Katie Smith on the 2007–2008 USA Women's Senior National Team in its bid for the 2008 Olympic Games in Beijing.

IN THEIR OWN WORDS

BECKY HAMMON

Five-time All-Star and fan favorite Becky Hammon of the San Antonio Silver Stars took time out during a whirlwind Washington, D.C., weekend ahead of the 2007 All-Star game to talk a little bit about what the support of WNBA fans means to the players and the league as it moves through its second decade.

The fans are the blood that runs the body of this league; to say they are essential is to understate their importance. We could not, and would not, exist without their support. Fans carried us through the first ten years and they will carry us through the second and beyond.

We have an extremely hard-core base in every city. They love you and follow you. It's great to meet with them, interact with them—and that relationship has been one of the trademarks of the league.

Of course as the league gets bigger in the future, the harder it will get to maintain that closeness, but there is no doubt that the WNBA fans will always be one of the most important elements of the league, and the players know that.

12. SUE WICKS

New York Liberty
#23, Forward
November 26, 1966

Wicks began her run into the women's basketball history books during her collegiate career with Rutgers University (1984–1988), where she was named Player of the Year for the Atlantic 10 Conference three consecutive years (1986–1988) and Atlantic 10 Tournament Most Valuable Player in 1986 and 1988. By the time she left Rutgers, Wicks held the Rutgers records for points scored (2,655), rebounds (1,357), scoring average (21.2 points per game), rebounds average (10.9 per game), field goals attempted and made (2,099 and 1,091), free throws attempted and made (641 and 473), and blocked shots (293). Her scoring and rebounding totals set records for a male or female player at Rutgers, and she was inducted into the Rutgers Hall of Fame in 1994.

Wicks spent several years overseas, playing professionally in Israel, Italy, Japan, and Spain before returning home for the inaugural WNBA draft, where she was selected by the Liberty and spent six seasons with them. Wicks was also the first WNBA player to publicly declare her sexual orientation.

13. LISA LESLIE

Los Angeles Sparks
#9, Center
July 7, 1972

Leslie has been a main fixture of the Sparks program since the WNBA's inaugural game on June 21, 1997. She has a 17.6 points and 9.3 rebounds per game average through the 2006 season, with her highest season points average of twenty coming in 2006. Leslie's scoring and dominant personality helped lead the Sparks to two WNBA Championships in 2001 and 2002, and playoff appearances in every season up through 2006. A three-time WNBA Most Valuable Player (2001, 2004, and 2006) and winner of the 2004 Defensive Player of the Year, Leslie was the first player to reach five thousand points in the league and the first woman to score a one-handed slam dunk in the WNBA on July 30, 2002.

Leslie is also one of three women, alongside Sheryl Swoopes and Dawn Staley, to win three consecutive Olympic gold medals.

14. CANDICE DUPREE

Chicago Sky
#4, Forward
August 16, 1984

The six-foot-two Tampa, Florida, native played 113 games in her collegiate career at Temple University, averaging fifteen points and 8.3 rebounds per game over four seasons while earning a degree in kinesiology. Dupree scored a double-double off the court with back-to-back nods in 2005 and 2006 as the Atlantic 10 Conference Player of the Year and Defensive Player of the Year.

The Chicago Sky snagged the former volleyball player during the first round of the 2006 draft as the sixth pick overall. Dupree went on to average 16.5 points and 7.7 rebounds per game in her 2007 rookie WNBA season, with her first appearance in an All-Star game as a reserve on the Eastern Conference team.

15. SEIMONE AUGUSTUS ("MONE")

Minnesota Lynx
#33, Guard
April 30, 1984

As a guard with Louisiana State, Augustus helped lead the Lady Tigers to the 2003 Southeastern Conference Tournament, two back-to-back NCAA Elite Eight appearances in 2004 and 2005, and on to the NCAA Final Four in 2005.

The Minnesota Lynx selected Augustus as the number-one draft pick ahead of the 2006 season and the Baton Rouge, Louisiana, native lost no time making her presence felt in the league. Augustus averaged 21.9 points per game and an .897 free throw percentage rate on her way to taking home 2006 Rookie of the Year honors.

Augustus has made back-to-back All-Star appearances in 2006 and 2007, was a member of the 2006 bronze medal–winning World Championship team, and looks to add an Olympic medal to her resume with an appearance in the 2008 Beijing Olympic Games.

15. KIM PERROT

Houston Comets
#10, Guard
January 18, 1967–August 19,1999

Perrot finished up her college career holding twenty-six records at the University of Southwestern Louisiana, and played six seasons overseas in Sweden, Germany, Israel, and France before returning home in 1997 to join the WNBA as one of its premier players. The five-foot-five point guard quickly ascended to the Houston Comets starting lineup and became a fan favorite for her ferocious and determined play that helped lead the Comets to two back-to-back WNBA Championships. Perrot averaged 8.5 points and 4.7 assists in the 1998 season, her last with the WNBA before being diagnosed with lung cancer in February 1999.

Throughout her battle with cancer and up until just weeks before her August 19, 1999, passing, the thirty-two-year-old continued to make public appearances and urge young girls to follow their dreams. Her will to fight both on and off the court remains a beacon for WNBA players and fans to this day. Perrot's teammates honored her memory with a posthumous presentation of a 1999 WNBA Championship ring and retired her jersey. Comets fans joined forces with the team to help raise money to create "Kim's Place," an area at the University of Texas M. D. Anderson Cancer Center in Houston where kids with cancer can play, relax, and visit with family members.

The then league president Val Ackerman honored Perrot "as a woman of great heart and indomitable courage who refused to be daunted by any challenge."* The WNBA subsequently renamed its annual sportsmanship award after the fallen Comet. More recently, Perrot was posthumously inducted into the Louisiana Sports Hall of Fame in June 2007.

15. TAJ MCWILLIAMS-FRANKLIN ("MOM")

Los Angeles Sparks
#3, Forward-Center
October 20, 1970

El Paso, Texas, born McWilliams-Franklin followed a solid college career at St. Edwards University, with three years in the American Basketball League playing for the Richmond–Philadelphia Rage before being selected by the

---

*"Kim Perrot dead at age 32"; August 20, 1999; Associated Press through CNN/SI.com, www.sportsillustrated.cnn.com/basketball/wnba/news/1999/08/19/obit_perrot_ap/.

Orlando Miracle in the third round of the 1999 draft. A dominant power forward with a penchant for double-doubles, McWilliams-Franklin traveled with the team when it developed into the Connecticut Sun, and reigned there as the team's official "Mom" until traded to Los Angeles ahead of the 2007 season, in the hopes she could provide experienced leadership after the departure of longtime Spark Tamecka Dixon and the absence of pregnant star center Lisa Leslie. She has spent the off-seasons playing for a diverse list of teams in countries including South Korea, the Czech Republic, Italy, Greece, and Spain.

When not playing basketball or taking care of her two daughters, McWilliams-Franklin can be found honoring her other passion—the written word. She reads an average of ten books a month (hopefully, at some point, including this one . . .) and writes poetry and short stories.

Thus far in her career the six-foot-two forward-center has played in two back-to-back WNBA Championships, in 2003 and 2004, had playoff appearances five years since 1999, and is a five-time All-Star. McWilliams-Franklin has averaged 12.4 points per game in the regular season over her WNBA years, with a career high 13.9 points per game average in the 2006 season.

Among her many accomplishments, McWilliams-Franklin was also a member of the 1998 World Championship gold medal team, the 2005 recipient of the Kim Perrot Sportsmanship Award, and is a member of the squad representing the United States at the 2008 Beijing Olympics.

ELEVEN

Community Outreach

From very early on the WNBA has put a premium on community outreach programs, operating both in partnership with the NBA and on its own, through established programs and in response to unfolding current national and world events. While community activism certainly helps increase league recognition from a marketing standpoint, many of the coaches, players, and WNBA insiders believe passionately in the issues and willingly devote their time above and beyond official events. Many of the players feel an understandable affinity for the struggles their young female fans are facing and will go out of their way to help, sometimes developing long-term relationships with young fans that go far beyond participation in a fitness clinic and an autograph.

Individual teams and players have adopted outreach projects in line with the WNBA's core programs that reflect the cities and towns they work and live in. The Detroit Shock, for example, has run the Tip-A-Shock fund-raiser since 2002, where Shock players serve food and drinks to patrons at a local restaurant in exchange for one-dollar tips to raise money for the March of

Dimes. Indiana Fever and the Big Brother, Big Sisters of Central Indiana have partnered to create the Fever Friends program, which pairs youngsters with adult mentors to attend WNBA games and interact with Fever players and coaching staff.

Besides the work done as part of the WNBA's official community outreach programs, or with their teams, many of the WNBA players contribute to the communities in their team's city and/or in their hometowns through

Juliette Terzieff

Young participants in WNBA BE Tour events in Washington, D.C., July 14, 2007 get tips from WNBA legend Jennifer Azzi.

individual efforts. Some players have gone on to form their own foundations, through which they aim to affect the lives of young people by helping them to overcome challenges in the hopes of winning a better future.

WNBA CARES

The core element of the league's community outreach efforts, WNBA Cares operates as part of NBA Cares, launched in 2005 to team up women's and men's basketball stars in a bid to provide over one hundred million hours of volunteer services to communities across the globe, help raise and contribute one hundred million dollars to charity, and build over one hundred places for kids to learn and play by 2010.

Most of the WNBA Cares programs are designed around the ideas of promoting health and fitness, and improving youth education and development with a variety of partners that include the American Heart Association, Feed the Children, Girls Inc., Habitat for Humanity, and Reading is Fundamental Inc.

The easiest way for fans—young and old alike—to find out about participating in or supporting any of the programs below, is to visit their local team's Web site for event announcements or through participation in local community organizations, with the exception of the Jr. NBA/Jr. WNBA programs, for which information is readily available at www.nba.com/jrnba/.

Breast Health Awareness

One of the league's earliest and most enduring programs, Breast Health Awareness is focused exclusively on raising awareness and education among young girls and women about breast cancer with the aim of boosting early detection rates. Events associated with the program have included in-arena nights, an annual Breast Health auction of WNBA merchandise and memorabilia, and sales of Breast Health Awareness T-shirts. Players who have personally been touched by cancer, including Katie Douglas, Rebecca Lobo, Lisa Leslie, and breast cancer survivor and program's national spokesperson Edna Campbell, have all lent their voices, ears, and shoulders to this program. The league and its players, working in partnership with the Susan G. Komen Breast Cancer Foundation since 2003, have raised over two million dollars to support the National Breast Cancer Alliance.

Jr. WNBA

The Jr. NBA/Jr. WNBA program, supported by Gatorade and Nike, provides support programs for coaches, players, parents, and officials participating in recreational youth leagues across the country and around the world. Events associated with this program include instructional programs, basketball camps and clinics, essay contests, and a season complete with a championship series. WNBA superstars Sue Bird and Tina Thompson, coach Bill Laimbeer, and official Lisa Mattingly are on the program's advisory council, while dozens of other WNBA players, coaches, and officials participate in events. This program helps support the efforts of more than five hundred thousand players a year from around the globe.

Read to Achieve

A joint NBA-WNBA program that operates year-round, reaching several million children every year, Read to Achieve looks to boost literacy rates and promote reading and online literacy as part of the pathway to success. Events associated with this program include thousands of reading-centered events every year, the donation of books, computers, and other literacy materials, and support for the creation of Learning Centers and Reading Corners. Since the program's launch in 2001, Read to Achieve associated programs have helped create more than one hundred Learning Centers and one hundred fifty Reading Corners, and donated more than seven hundred fifty thousand books and magazines.

WNBA Be Smart-Be Fit-Be Yourself

This year-round program seeks to emphasize knowledge of one's body and healthy living through a series of activities related to nutrition, health, fitness, and self-esteem. Events associated with this program include fitness clinics, Be Fit Journals, contests, and a WNBA BE Tour mobile fitness fair that travels around the country in support of the program. WNBA stars, including Jennifer Azzi, Monique Currie, Diana Taurasi, and program spokesperson Betty Lennox are often featured in the events.

WNBA ACTION ON BROADER ISSUES

The WNBA has also proven its willingness to reach beyond the normal scope of basketball-related outreach in response to public need in the United States and around the world. When Hurricane Katrina carved a swathe of unprecedented storm destruction in 2005, the NBA, WNBA, and their teams committed two million dollars to the relief effort. Among the many laudable efforts from within the league that followed, the Connecticut Sun donated over seventy-one thousand dollars of ticket sales, fan donations, and a silent auction conducted around a September 2005 playoff game against the Detroit Shock, and the Houston Comets worked alongside the Rockets and other local businesses to conduct a three-day HopeFest in Houston, Texas, to collect and distribute donations and help evacuees find jobs and housing.

On the international stage the league has joined the ongoing efforts of some of the world's leading philanthropists and nongovernmental organizations to tackle persistent issues that plague millions.

Sports Illustrated columnist Rick Reilly somewhat inadvertently kicked off the global grassroots antimalaria campaign Nothing But Nets in a May 2006 article, where he challenged readers to make a ten-dollar donation to purchase and distribute an insecticide-treated bed net to a family in need. Malaria infects five hundred million people every year, killing a million of them. Ninety percent of those deaths occur in Africa. Reilly's column received such overwhelming support that the journalist teamed up with the United Nations Foundation to expand the project, and Nothing But Nets was born.

NBA Cares, WNBA Cares, VH1, AOL Black Voices, and Major League Soccer's MLS W.O.R.K.S. emerged as partner organizations in the effort, joining thousands of people from around the world who have been raising money in their communities and schools through everything from bake sales to performance art. For the WNBA, the participation has included in-

IN THEIR OWN WORDS

TAMIKA CATCHINGS

Indiana Fever forward Tamika Catchings, founder and president of the Catch the Stars Foundation, talks about why she believes giving back to the community helps keep her grounded and is an essential part of her basketball career. Catchings also believes that having found success, these star athletes can honor and give something back to the people who helped their careers.

The concept of community outreach means being out in the community and being able to make a difference and a huge impact in the community around you—in my foundation's case to provide our youth with positive academic and sports-related programs that will help them catch their dreams one star at a time.

For me, knowing that I'm able to make a positive impact on those around me and allowing these kids to get one step closer to their dreams and their goals is the thing that keeps me going.

I think that all of my community outreach is a reflection of how I grew up and the people that have been in my life. Plenty of times we attended arena and public events that feature public service announcements, distribution of informational materials, efforts to honor local contributors from the communities, and player testimonials.

In January 2007 the Bill and Melinda Gates Foundation provided a challenge grant that would match dollar-for-dollar all contributions up to $3 million. As of July 2007 the campaign had raised $7 million, enough for seven hundred thousand bed nets in its quest to eventually provide the three hundred million treated bed nets needed worldwide.

The WNBA has also partnered with CARE at in-arena and public events

different outreach events with our parents while we were growing up, and I think of all of the people that have been in my life that have wanted to see me succeed, and that encouraged me to keep striving forward.

There's nothing more magical than living in a world where there are so many supportive people around you.

It's always great to have public face recognition behind programs because it helps to advance programs, and it almost becomes a double positive in the community. After all, all of us were given opportunities through different roads and different people that have been involved in our lives—and not all of those people were getting paid to make a difference.

I think of all of the young kids that started in our programs and have grown to be successful in whatever walk of life they've chosen. I think about the smiles that are put on kids' faces even when, on some days, I may not have started off being in the mood to do anything.

to battle global poverty. CARE, one of the world's most well-known humanitarian groups, operates community-based programs in over seventy countries promoting education, economic self-sufficiency, and health care, with a particular focus on empowering women. In March 2007, Washington Mystics owner Sheila Johnson joined with CARE to help launch the "I Am Powerful" campaign, a national effort to encourage women in the United States to actively engage to improve the lives of impoverished women around the world. The project has drawn support from other big name ambassadors including Meg Ryan, Anne Hathaway, and Atlanta Mayor Shirley Franklin. Johnson has offered $5 million to jump start the project, the bulk of which is slated to be used to match donations from the public dollar-for-dollar.

PLAYER FOUNDATIONS

Many of the programs run by players' foundations, like the Dawn Staley Foundation, are open to public participation, and information for those interested is best found on their Web sites or by contacting the foundation directly. Other foundations, such as Cash for Kids, provide funding to augment the efforts of schools, community groups, shelters, and other children-focused organizations. More information is always available on the players' and foundations' Web sites. Almost every year WNBA players set up new foundations or increase their initiatives, but here is a sample of what some of the women of the WNBA are doing in their communities.

Betty Ann Robinson (BAR) Foundation
Nakia Sanford
www.thebarfoundation.com

Founded in 2005 by Nakia Sanford in memory of her late grandmother, Betty Ann Robinson, the BAR Foundation aims to contribute to a solid support system for youngsters as they approach adulthood. Sanford, a Decatur, Georgia, native, has competed for teams in Italy, Belgium, Turkey, and France, among others, and now features prominently on the Washington Mystics roster as a forward/center.

Select program details

e-Sisters Mentoring Program: An e-mail-based mentorship program pairing high school students with professional adults, featuring regular e-mail communication and outings once a month aimed at increasing youngsters' computer, writing, and communication skills.

Girl Talk: An outreach program of peer-dominated focus groups in which young girls can discuss topics they may not feel comfortable broaching with parents or teachers, in the hopes of decreasing any feelings of isolation young participants may be feeling.

Kia's Kids: Gives youngsters a chance to write to Sanford and tell her what special things they are doing in the summer months, with some getting tickets to a Washington Mystics game.

Bowling with the Stars Fund-raisers: Sanford brings together public figures to participate in bowling matches against members of the general public in Washington, D.C., as a means to raise money to support the Foundation's efforts.

For more information:

Tepricka Morgan

Bickerstaff Sports & Entertainment

2828 10th Street, NE

Washington, D.C. 20017

202-832-8560 Tel

info@thebarfoundation.org

Cash for Kids
Swin Cash
www.swincash.com/cashforkids/cfkmission.html

Founded in 2004, the foundation aims to help provide children with the skills necessary to excel in school and on the court through foundation-run programs and financial contributions supporting programs in the arts, youth development, and athletics run by youth agencies and schools in the Detroit, Michigan, and McKeesport, Pennsylvania, areas. Cash, a forward for the Detroit Shock, turned pro in 2002 and has since gone on to be a member of the 2003 and 2006 WNBA Championship teams, a two-time WNBA All-Star, and to win Olympic gold.

Select program details

Strive with Pride Basketball Clinics: Free basketball clinics at the Swin Cash Recreation City in McKeesport, Pennsylvania, begun by Cash's mother, Cynthia, and hosted annually by Cash herself.

It's Your Life Retreats: A new program to be launched in 2008 of one-day-long retreats for the mind, body, and soul to be held in both the Pittsburgh, Pennsylvania, and Detroit, Michigan, areas aimed at helping young girls develop self-confidence and healthy lifestyles.

Ferguson Academy for Young Women in Detroit: One of many projects supported by the foundation, Cash for Kids joined with the Detroit Shock to build a state-of-the-art resource center for the Ferguson Academy, one of only a handful of American schools that allow young mothers to bring their children to school with them and provide day care facilities on site.

Game Tickets: For every Detroit Shock home game, the foundation donates thirty-two tickets and "Cash for Kids" T-shirts to underprivileged youth.

For more information:

Donyale Martin, Director of Executive Affairs

2939 South Rochester Rd., Suite 190

Rochester Hills, MI 48307
dmartin@swincash.com

Catch the Stars Foundation
Tamika Catchings
www.catchin24.com/foundation.asp

Founded in 2004, Catch the Stars Foundation aims to motivate and guide at-risk youth in the Indianapolis area through academic and sports-related programs. Catchings, a New Jersey native, joined the WNBA's Indiana Fever in 2001, was subsequently named Rookie of the Year, and is an Olympic gold medalist.

Select program details

Catch on to Fitness Clinics: Fitness clinics focusing on proper nutrition and exercise for youth aged seven to fourteen, for which admission is ten canned goods items that go to a local food bank.

Holiday Basketball Camp: A three-day annual event held in December open to boys and girls aged nine to fourteen, featuring basketball demonstrations and drills, and an end-of-camp buffet dinner attended by participants and their families.

STARS/CHAMPS: Eight-week programs, STARS for girls and CHAMPS for boys, focused on goal setting, building self-esteem, and decision-making skills and career planning.

Catchings Corner: A community ticket block purchased by the foundation for every Indiana Fever home game, which gives away blocks of sixteen tickets to local children's clubs.

For more information:
Tauja Catchings
317-329-8424 Tel
catchthestars24@aol.com

Dawn Staley Foundation
Dawn Staley
www.dawnstaley5.com

Founded in 1996, the foundation seeks to provide opportunities for at-risk youth through education and sports focused programs in the Philadelphia, Pennsylvania, area. Staley is an Olympic gold medalist and professional athlete who played for the WNBA's Charlotte Sting and Houston Comets before retiring in 2006.

Select program details

Dawn Staley Foundation After School Program: A program for fifty middle school students a year that includes computer and reading programs, mentoring, health education, workshops, and community outreach activities.

Summer Basketball League and Mentoring Program: A summer program featuring organized games, developmental clinics, and mentoring for one hundred girls a season aimed at teaching the importance of teamwork and good sportsmanship.

Day in the Park Celebration: An annual event in north Philadelphia featuring food, music, and entertainment designed to promote civic pride and family interaction.

For more information:

5230 N. Broad Street
Philadelphia, PA 19141
215-457-1270 Tel
215-457-1817 Fax
dawnstaleyfoundation@yahoo.com

Diana Taurasi Foundation
Diana Taurasi
www.dianataurasi.com

Taurasi's foundation was still in its formulative stages in 2007, but that didn't stop the Mercury star from headlining projects aimed at giving youngsters a better shot at improving their future. Taurasi helped lead the University of Connecticut to three straight NCAA titles and took home an Olympic gold medal at the 2004 Athens games, before joining the WNBA's Phoenix Mercury as the 2005 WNBA number-one draft pick. Taurasi went on to become Rookie of the Year, was voted to the All-Star game three times in a row, and helped Phoenix bring home the 2007 WNBA Championship title.

Select program details

Kid's Playground, Bridgeport, Connecticut: The foundation partnered with KaBoom!, a national nonprofit organization advocating for safe play areas within walking distance of every child, and local donors to build a children's playground in October 2006.

Learn and Player Center: Taurasi called on All-Star friends Cappie Pondexter, Sue Bird, and Lauren Jackson in July 2007 to help her raise funds for a learning center to benefit the Boys and Girls Club in Guadalupe, a Native American and Hispanic community near Phoenix, due to open in November 2008. To decrease a dropout rate of over 75 percent in the community, Taurasi hopes the center will provide extra opportunities and encourage more kids to stay in school.

For more information:

Lindsay Kagawa

BDA Sports Management

822 Ashley Lane, Suite A

Walnut Creek, CA 94597

lkagawa@bdasports.com

Lennox Foundation 22
Betty Lennox
www.lennox22.org

Founded in 2005, the foundation aims to help abused, neglected, and under-privileged children experience positive developments in their lives by delivering support, education, and self-motivation through basketball. Most of the foundation's programs support shelters and homes in an effort to bolster their existing programs. Lennox was named Rookie of the Year her inaugural WNBA season with Minnesota in 2000, subsequently playing a season each in Miami and Cleveland before joining the Seattle Storm in 2003, then going on to become the WNBA Finals Most Valuable Player in the Storm's 2004 championship winning season.

Select program details

New Beginnings Backpack Drive: In summer 2006 the foundation collected backpacks filled with back-to-school supplies that were then given to needy children through the Seattle area New Beginnings program. The foundation subsequently supplied New Beginnings, which provides shelter, support groups, and other services for abused women and children, with computers, clothing, and other supplies.

Basketball Camps: The foundation runs basketball camps in Seattle and Kansas City to benefit the operations of New Beginnings, and Missouri's Hope House, which runs a hotline and domestic violence programs that aid fifteen thousand women and children every year.

For more information:

The Lennox Foundation 22
13701 42nd Ave., NE
Seattle, WA 98125
lcole@lennox22.org
b-money@lennox22.org

TWENTY Foundation
Tamika Williams
www.tamikawilliams.org

The TWENTY (Tamika Williams Energizes and Nurtures Today's Youth) Foundation seeks to help develop leaders of the future by engaging the youth of today to develop life skills in the Dayton, Ohio, area, and hopes to have a recreation and wellness center to nurture the health, bodies, and minds of families built by its ten-year anniversary. The foundation runs several educational, sports, and mentoring programs. Williams, a Dayton native, began her professional career with a 2002 draft selection to the Minnesota Lynx and is now a team captain.

Select program details

Tamika Williams Girls Developmental Basketball League: An eleven-week program of skills learning sessions, practices, team games, an All-Star game, and an awards banquet.

Tamika Williams HARDWORK Basketball Camp: A three-day program featuring in-depth drills, development of fundamental basketball skills, leadership lectures, shooting relays, and hotshot contests.

For more information:

Junie Harris

Director, Client Development

Bickerstaff Sports & Entertainment

jharris@bsesports.net

TWELVE

Forging Connections

Fans of the WNBA get only a few short months a year to watch their favorite players battle it out on the way the WNBA Championship Series, but that doesn't mean true women's basketball aficionados are left with nothing to do during the off season. From watching NCAA players (and keeping an ever-watchful eye for the next Seimone Augustus or Cappie Pondexter) to following along as WNBA players' fortunes unfold in overseas leagues or in their off-season coaching jobs, there is plenty to keep passionate fans sated until the draft season really ramps up some six months later.

For those just beginning their journey into the exciting world of the WNBA or looking to expand their knowledge of the game, this chapter provides a list of places to visit, either on the Web or in person, for everything from the day's latest news to a complete history of the women's game of basketball.

There's also a sample reading list designed to engage readers young and old alike. Those out there who are not long-time fans of women's hoops, as well as those out there who are, can all find inspiration and tips not only for basketball but for the game of life in the struggles, disappointments, and victories contained in the pages of the books on this reading list.

Some of the best information (and biggest fun) can be found by visiting with and engaging other WNBA fans through their individual blogs or on boards where lively and (very, *very*) passionate debate is the accepted norm. There are devoutly dedicated fans in virtually every city where the WNBA has teams and most of them have an online presence. Not only do the fans collectively provide a wealth of information you're unlikely to find anywhere else, but their true passion for the players, the game, and the league is a testament to the league's ability to build on the successes of its first decade.

WOMEN'S BASKETBALL HALL OF FAME
700 HALL OF FAME DRIVE
KNOXVILLE, TN 37915
865-633-9000

Ask anyone who has been there and they will all say the same thing about a trip through the Women's Basketball Hall of Fame—it is *the* ultimate journey through the annals of women's hoops and a *must see* for any WNBA fan. Founded in 1999, the Hall features a host of permanent and temporary exhibits—some of which are detailed below—paying tribute to the history of the women's game and helping push forward hopes for its future.

Exhibitions

Visitors begin their journey inside with the State Farm Tip-Off theater featuring a fifteen-minute film "Hoopful of Hope" tracing women's basketball history back to 1892 up through the 1990s, before moving on to encounter an animatronics version of the mother of women's basketball, Senda Berenson, expressing her thoughts on the game's early days. A trip through

Neil Crosby, Neil Studios, Courtesy of the Women's Basketball Hall of Fame

The Knoxville, TN Hall of Fame is a must see for women's basketball fans.

locker rooms modeled in both the old style and the new follows, in which visitors can sit through a halftime speech from a rotating lineup of some of the game's leading coaches.

The Hall features dozens of memorabilia displays, including one of women's basketball's original 1901 rule books, the trophy the United States won at the 1957 World Championship, and the jersey worn by West Virginia University's Georgeann Wells when she became the first female player to dunk in a collegiate game. Hanging overhead is the Hall's Ring of Honor, a collection of over one hundred jerseys of high school and collegiate All-Americans and WNBA All-Stars. There are also photographic displays, exhibits of women's basketball notables like the All-American Red Heads, and a "Winners' Wall," which recognizes championship teams from grassroots organizations and collegiate teams up through the WNBA and the Olympics.

The Hall's final exhibit is the Hall of Honor, where individuals inducted into the Women's Basketball Hall of Fame are formally recognized. The 1999 inaugural class list of inductees included basketball luminaries Olympian

BASKETBALL BOOK LIST

The following list is a sampling of the titles available on the market that are related to women's basketball and the WNBA, which can be found at places like the Women's Basketball Hall of Fame and major booksellers, or online through various retailers such as Barnes & Noble and Amazon.com.

For extremely young or beginning readers:

J Is for Jump Shot: A Basketball Alphabet Mike Ulmer (Sleeping Bear Press, First Edition: August 2005)

> Synopsis: An introductory look at the game, fundamentals, famous players, and rules for readers aged four to eight. Part of the Sleeping Bear Press's series of sports alphabet titles.

The Princesses Have a Ball Teresa Bateman (Albert Whitman & Company, September 2002)

> Synopsis: An updated version of the classic story in which twelve princesses wear out their shoes every night not by dancing, but by playing basketball, until a cobbler designs special new shoes for the hoop-addicted royal offspring.

Salt in His Shoes: Michael Jordan in Pursuit of a Dream Deloris Jordan with Roslyn M. Jordan (Simon & Schuster Children's Publishing, November 2000)

> Synopsis: Long before his name became synonymous with unrivaled basketball greatness, a young Michael Jordan struggled to overcome a court bully and his lack of height, learning that determination and practice can make a winner.

Swish! Bill Martin Jr., Michael Sampson, and Michael Chesworth (Henry Holt and Co., September 1997)

> Synopsis: Tells the fictional story of the hotly contested final minutes of a girl's basketball game between the Cardinals and the Blue Jays.

For young readers:

Chamique Holdsclaw: My Story Chamique Holdsclaw and Jennifer Frey (Aladdin, April 2001)

> Synopsis: Holdsclaw—with the help of Jennifer Frey—tells the story of her personal journey from painful recollections of childhood family problems and strife over feeling like an outsider because of her sports prowess, to becoming the WNBA 1999 Rookie of the Year.

Hoop Girlz Lucy Jane Bledsoe (Holiday House, October 2002)

> Synopsis: A young girl with dreams of playing in the WNBA some-day forms her own team after trying out unsuccessfully for an existing team headed for a large tournament.

The Real Slam Dunk Charisse K. Richardson (Puffin Books, Penguin Group, February 2005)

> Synopsis: Richardson introduces basketball-loving twins Mia and Marcus, and follows their story as Marcus learns that success on the court is only complete when complemented by successes off the court.

The Real Lucky Charm Charisse K. Richardson (Puffin Books, Penguin Group, September 2005)

> Synopsis: Picking up on the story of basketball-loving twins Mia and Marcus, Mia learns important life lessons after overcoming the loss of a gold basketball charm from her bracelet to which she attributed her growing basketball and educational prowess.

Summer Ball Matt Lupica (Philomel, May 2007)

> Synopsis: Determination helps young player Danny Walker excel at summer basketball camp and lead his team to victory.

Teresa Weatherspoon's Basketball for Girls Teresa Weatherspoon
(Jossey-Bass, 1999)

> Synopsis: In this instructional tome, basketball legend Teresa Weatherspoon lays out practical advice—and her own personal tips and secrets—for success on the court through a series of exercises designed to help players master basketball fundamentals.

For other readers:

Basketball for Women: Becoming a Complete Player Nancy Lieberman-Cline and Robin Roberts (Human Kinetics Publishers, November 1995)

> Synopsis: Women's basketball legend Lieberman-Cline teams up with Roberts, a college player who went on to sports broadcasting, to bring readers a comprehensive playbook, including drills and conditioning programs to help players fulfill their potential.

Just for Fun—The Story of AAU Women's Basketball Robert W. Ikard (University of Arkansas Press, March 2005)

> Synopsis: A history of the female players, coaches, and teams who participated in the American Athletic Union's women's basketball programs as amateurs at a time when there were few opportunities for female basketball players.

Reach for the Summit Pat Summitt with Sally Jenkins (Broadway Books, March 1998)

> Synopsis: Legendary University of Tennessee coach Pat Summitt lays out her twelve commandments for lasting success in life, sports, and business.

Raise the Roof   Pat Summitt (Broadway Books, October 1999)

Synopsis: Legendary University of Tennessee coach Pat Summit takes readers on a journey through the team's 1997–98 campaign when the Lady Vols went 39–0 and won their third straight NCAA Championship.

Shattering the Glass: The Remarkable History of Women's Basketball   Pamela Grundy and Susan Shackelford (New Press, August 2005)

Synopsis: An extensive history of women's basketball from the game's inception through the formation of the WNBA, written by two sportswriters who examine the resistance women have faced in their quest to play.

Strong Women, Deep Closets: Lesbians and Homophobia in Sports   Pat Griffin (Human Kinetics Publishers, February 1998)

Synopsis: Former athlete and coach Griffin examines the stereotypes and prejudice associated with women's sports and lesbianism, the difficulties lesbian athletes encounter, and strategies to deal with the situation.

She Got Game–My Personal Odyssey   Cynthia Cooper (Warner Books, June 2000)

Synopsis: Legendary basketballer Cooper tells her own inspirational story of overcoming poverty and personal insecurities to rise to the top of women's basketball.

Special thanks to the Women's Basketball Hall of Fame for their contributions of book titles and recommended reading lists.

Nancy Lieberman, pioneering coach Carol Eckman, Soviet player Uljana Semjonova, and Korean player Shin-Ja Park. Forty-two-year career coach Dan Weese, Houston Comets coach Van Chancellor, and two-time Olympian Lynette Woodard are among those subsequently honored as inductees over the last eight years.

At the back of the building, visitors will see something present nowhere else on the planet: the world's only thirty-foot-tall, ten-ton basketball sitting atop a glass staircase in the shape of a basketball net.

Interactive Components

There are several interactive features to keep visitors in the game during their visit. In the Hall's downstairs area visitors can compare and sharpen their shooting, dribbling, and passing skills in three interactive displays. At the tip-off interactive, for example, visitors can measure and compare their vertical leap to those of WNBA legends Lisa Leslie and Cynthia Cooper. The downstairs basketball court also features baskets at three heights—the original height of eight feet, the present height of nine feet, and a projected future height of ten—where visitors can literally feel the game's historical progression through their own shots. Visitors can also stop by the "I'm in the Hall" area where a computer kiosk is set up to allow fans to take their picture and see themselves appear on the Halls' Web site.

The Hall also has an extensive gift shop, called Trophies, where fans can find Hall of Fame apparel, inductee-signed basketballs, a wide range of accessories, and books on the women's game.

Special Events

Every year, usually in June, the Hall hosts an induction ceremony for a class of six inductees selected from a pool of public-nominated candidates from three categories—player, coach, and contributor. The Hall sells tickets to the ceremony, and there is a free inductee autograph session open to the public.

For details on specific events fans should check out the Hall's Web site or call the Hall.

Visiting Remotely

For those who can't physically make the trip to Knoxville, the Women's Basketball Hall of Fame maintains a Web site (www.wbhof.com) with information on the Hall itself, inductees, merchandise available for purchase online, history of the game, and a FAQ's section.

Other Information

The Women's Basketball Hall of Fame runs a Sportsmanship Program introduced in 2005 that focuses on teaching coaches, parents, and young athletes how to be good sports. The program's main component is a booklet including sportsmanship statistics, fundamentals of good sportsmanship, vocabulary, and scenario exercises. Participants sign a code of conduct pledging to be a good sport. While the Hall's efforts are geared primarily toward its own geographical area, individuals interested in participating can call the Hall for more information or to request participation pamphlets.

For those who can get there, portions of the Hall are also available to host weddings, business meetings, and basketball team celebrations. The Hall also has birthday party packages that include playing time on the Hall's Urban Playground, admission into the Hall of Fame, paper products, and table decorations. Contact Dana Hart at 865-633-9000, extension 225 for more information on facility rentals.

BASKETBALL BLOGS AND FAN BOARDS

Chasing the Title
www.stormdefense.blogspot.com

Self-described basketball addict Patrick Sheehy blogs his thoughts, commentary, and analysis on the Seattle Storm and the WNBA. Sheehy, also a number-crunching fan, provides a link to pages with league and individual team annual defensive and offensive statistics dating back to the league's inaugural 1997 season.

DC Basketcases
www.dcbasketcases.blogspot.com/

This self-proclaimed "friendly asylum for a couple of crazy D.C.-area women's basketball fans" is maintained by Mystics and Terps lovers Eileen and Judith, who post pre- and postgame analyses, opinions, and news associated with women's basketball, and provide access to a searchable archive dating back to May 2006.

Gotnext Women's Basketball Boards
Home of the Phoenix Mercury Message Board
www.gotnext.com/index.php

This board has threads for discussions on the Mercury, the WNBA, and Arizona State University topics, with archives available and a link to Mercury memorabilia and items for sale on eBay.

Minnesota Women's Basketball Forums
www.mnwomensbb.shortstreet.net/phpBB2/index.php

Bulletin board administrator Sue Short has created a forum for fans of the Minnesota Women's Gophers, the Minnesota Lynx, and Minnesota high school girl's basketball, which also features archived discussions of thread highlights from past seasons.

Off Court
www.off-court.com

Creator Abigail Hull has fashioned a Web site dedicated to the discussion of women's basketball. With commentaries written by contributors, including Melissa Sterry, David Siegel, and WNBA legend Kym Hampton, Off Court provides in-depth discourse on the game from people who love and understand its many intricacies. The site will also accept publishable commentary from readers and members of the basketball community, and is looking to create what Hull aims to be the most concise and comprehensive database of professional, national, and college basketball team links.

Rebkell's Junkie Boards
www.boards.rebkell.net

Board owner Robert Lingerfelt hosts discussions on both men's and women's NCAA, NBA, and WNBA basketball. While Rebkell's most popular threads are undoubtedly the WNBA forum followed by the WCBB—women's college basketball forum, one of Rebkell's most interesting threads is WNBA Collectibles, where fans can barter, arrange purchase, or find links and discussions to places selling WNBA merchandise and memorabilia.

She's Got Game
Women's Hoops and Nothin' but the Hoops
www.shesgotgame.blogspot.com

Blogger Steve Rice includes coverage of everything from WNBA breaking news and trends and NCAA happenings, to off-the-court news items of interest to basketball fans. She's Got Game features links to WNBA and NCAA headlines from major U.S. national news sources, posts archives back to January 2005, and a long list of other women's basketball Web sites, forums, and blogs.

Stormtracker
www.seattlestorm.blogspot.com

This blog, penned by Kevin Pelton for the last five seasons, is the Seattle Storm's official blog featuring reports from team practices, Storms breaking news, and analysis of the Storm and the WNBA.

WNBA Fan Voice
www.wnba.com/index.jspa

The WNBA Web site hosts a fan forum for those who "live, breathe, and dream WNBA basketball 24/7/365" with discussion areas for general WNBA chatter and team-focused thoughts as well as a "Coaches Corner" where strategy comparisons dominate. WNBA Fan Voice also hosts Game Date forums that open from the start of the first game every day of the season.

WNBA Fan Voice Blogs
www.wnba.com/category.jspa?categoryID=7

WNBA Fan Voice hosts about a dozen regular bloggers, including WNBA president Donna Orender, basketball legend Rebecca Lobo, WNBA.com's editor

Adam Hirshfield, and a roster of official WNBA.com fan bloggers, including Georgia-based Kevin, Tammy from Texas, and Rebecca from New York.

WNBATalk.com
www.wnbatalk.com

WNBATalk.com, described by its administrators as a central gathering place for fans to discuss the "league that they love," is a fan forum message board with threads on the league, players, teams, and overall season impressions, with a section for threads on non-WNBA topics.

Women's Hoops Blog
Inane commentary on a sport that deserves far better
www.womenshoops.blogspot.com

Women's Hoops Blog, founded by Ted and Sara Sampsell-Jones in 2003, features links to mainstream media stories plus analysis and commentary from the founders as well as dedicated contributors Stephen "Steve" Burt, Jessica Bennet, and Helen Wheelock. The blog is updated throughout the day. The site also features a comprehensive list of blogs, boards, and general basketball links, as well as archives dating back to February 2003.

BASKETBALL AND BASKETBALL MAGAZINE WEB SITES

Full Court Press
www.fullcourt.scout.com/?refid=4740

Full Court Press covers all levels of women's basketball, from high school to international, and has done so since 1996, offering perspective and analysis by a roster of regular contributors.

Gball—For girls who play basketball
www.gballmag.com

Gball has plenty to offer younger basketball players and fans including a link to sign up for the Gball Club biweekly newsletter, a searchable database of basketball camps, latest WNBA news, a Let's Chat section with a site-generated question-and-answer from other Gball users, and a Gmall stocked with basketball gear.

Girls Hoops
www.girlshoops.scout.com

Devoted to high school and college basketball, Girls Hoops covers news, information on scouting, and maintains forums for fans of the game.

Inside Hoops
www.insidehoops.com/wnba

Founded by journalist Jeffrey Lenchiner in 1999, Inside Hoops covers everything in, around, and about the basketball world (NBA, WNBA, college and high school hoops, UBSL, and Streetball) with news, rumors, original articles, and fan forums.

WBL Memories
www.wblmemories.com

This site is the result of devoted women's basketball fan Karra Porter's efforts to pay tribute to the short-lived Women's Professional Basketball League, America's first professional female basketball league. Porter, author of 2006's *Mad Seasons: The Story of the First Women's Basketball League* (University of Nebraska Press), has included a WBL history, player rosters, and team information.

Women's Basketball Coaches Association
www.wbca.org

While the WBCA's focus is to unite female coaches from all levels of the game in order to better promote women's basketball, its Web site has a wide array of information, including daily news, legislative events that affect women's basketball, and lists of events, camps, and clinics.

Women's Basketball Magazine
www.wbmagazine.com

Web site of the bimonthly periodical *Women's Basketball*, owned by Tampa, Florida–based Goldman Publishing, which covers the WNBA, college, and high school hoops through news and features. It is the only magazine as of summer 2007 that is dedicated solely to the sport of women's basketball, and also contains instructional articles as well as pieces on health and fitness.

Women's Basketball Online
Where women's basketball meets the Internet
womensbasketballonline.com

Womensbasketballonline.com, owned and operated by tireless women's hoops fan Kim Callahan, contains just about everything a WNBA fan could want. The site, founded in 1999, prominently features daily news links, original articles and opinion pieces, and television broadcast schedules, but is also home to a comprehensive collection of content including a women's basketball history timeline, a directory of links to more information on the WBNA, college basketball, and international basketball programs, and a month-by-month breakdown of players' and coaches' birthdays.

THIRTEEN

Multiple-Choice Game

Now that we're almost at the end, everyone should have a pretty good handle on the WNBA and women's basketball. But we're not about to let you leave without a little game of our own special brand of hoops just to make sure. Most of the answers can be found somewhere in the other chapters of this book; a few cannot (nod and bow to the WNBA fanatics out there who bought this guide), but go ahead and take your best shot anyway! Sure, you could cheat and look at the answer section at the end of this chapter, but that'd take the fun out of it. And besides, if you circle your answers in pencil nobody need ever know which questions you got wrong.

Every standard correct answer scores you a basket (2 points) and wrong answers earn you a big ole goose egg (0 points). But watch out for the trick questions—get them right and you've scored a three-pointer (3 points). Add up your scores at the end and see how you rank!

QUESTIONS

1. Who was the last original WNBA coach to leave his/her post?
    A. Cheryl Miller
    B. Van Chancellor
    C. Nancy Darsch
    D. Michael Cooper

2. Which of the following legendary women's basketball players was the first woman to play with a men's professional team?
    A. Anne Meyers-Drysdale
    B. Carol Blazejowski
    C. Nancy Lieberman
    D. Teresa Weatherspoon

3. Who was the first player to reach five thousand career points in the WNBA?
    A. Vickie Johnson
    B. Katie Smith
    C. Lisa Leslie
    D. Sheryl Swoopes

4. Which of the following countries have seen their nationals play for a WNBA team?
    A. Brazil
    B. Hungary
    C. Lithuania
    D. All of the above

5. Which of the following players have been named Rookie of the Year and won the WNBA Championship in the same year?
   A. Cheryl Ford
   B. Seimone Augustus
   C. Betty Lennox
   D. Diana Taurasi

6. Which of the following players have won three Olympic medals?
   A. Lisa Leslie
   B. Seimone Augustus
   C. Sheryl Swoopes
   D. Katie Smith

7. Which of the following were not among the original eight WNBA teams?
   A. Detroit Shock
   B. Seattle Storm
   C. Charlotte Sting
   D. Houston Comets

8. Which of the following players were responsible for the "WNBA Greatest Moment"?
   A. Chamique Holdsclaw
   B. Teresa Weatherspoon
   C. Cynthia Cooper
   D. Shay Doron

9. How many WNBA All-Star games has the Western Conference won?

  A. Five

  B. Six

  C. Seven

  D. Eight

10. Which of the following players were number-one draft picks?

  A. Margo Dydek

  B. Diana Taurasi

  C. Ann Wauters

  D. All of the above

11. Which of the following women's basketball legends was the first woman to play with the Harlem Globetrotters?

  A. Lynette Woodard

  B. Joyce Walker

  C. Nancy Lieberman

  D. Margaret Wade

12. Which player was the first to record a WNBA triple-double?

  A. Lisa Leslie

  B. Margo Dydek

  C. Deanna Nolan

  D. Sheryl Swoopes

13. In which year was the game of basketball introduced for women?

  A. 1892

  B. 1896

  C. 1899

  D. 1901

14. Which of the following players did not feature on the 1998 WNBA Championship-winning Houston Comets team?

A. Cynthia Cooper

B. Sheryl Swoopes

C. Ruthie Bolton

D. Rebecca Lobo

15. Which of the following players did not feature on the 2007–08 squad for the USA Women's Senior National Team headed for the 2008 Beijing Olympics?

A. Tamika Catchings

B. Lindsey Harding

C. Alana Beard

D. Cappie Pondexter

16. Which of the following players was the Rookie of the Year for the 1997 season?

A. Tracy Reid

B. Chamique Holdsclaw

C. Betty Lennox

D. Kym Hampton

17. Which of the following is not a standard basketball term?

A. Full-court press

B. Take-n-run

C. Give-and-go

D. Outlet pass

18. Which player won the WNBA's first-ever tip-off?

   A. Kym Hampton

   B. Lisa Leslie

   C. Mwadi Mabika

   D. Vickie Johnson

19. Who was the first non-U.S. player drafted into the WNBA?

   A. Tammy Sutton-Brown

   B. Lauren Jackson

   C. Tully Bevilaqua

   D. Margo Dydek

20. In which year did the USA Women's Senior National Team not win a medal at the Olympics?

   A. 1976

   B. 1980

   C. 1988

   D. 1992

21. Which player holds the most responsibility for getting the ball downcourt?

   A. Center

   B. Power forward

   C. Point guard

   D. Shooting guard

22. Which of the following characteristics did all the members of the 2006 WNBA All-Decade Team share?

   A. WNBA Champion

   B. Olympic medal winner

   C. Top ten all-time scorers

   D. None of the above

23. Which of the following is not a defensive tactic?

   A. Half-court press

   B. Man-to-man

   C. Trap

   D. Fast break

24. Which country's team was the first to beat the United States in Olympic competition?

   A. Bulgaria

   B. Canada

   C. Japan

   D. None of the above

25. With which of the following organizations does the WNBA partner as part of its community outreach efforts?

   A. American Heart Association

   B. March of Dimes

   C. Nothing But Nets

   D. All of the above

ANSWERS

1: B. Van Chancellor (2 points)

The last remaining original WNBA head coach, Van Chancellor resigned from the Houston Comets in January 2007 as the WNBA's most decorated coach, with four back-to-back WNBA Championship wins (1997–2000) and three back-to-back Coach of the Year wins (1997–1999). Van Chancellor is now the head coach at Louisiana State University.

Nancy Darsch was the New York Liberty's first coach. After two seasons, she moved on to lead the Washington Mystics and then to an assistant coach position with the Minnesota Lynx, before settling into her current position as assistant coach at Boston College.

Cheryl Miller coached the Phoenix Mercury from its inaugural 1997 season through the 2000 season, before moving on to work in broadcasting.

Michael Cooper joined the Los Angeles Sparks prior to the 1999 season as an assistant coach. Named head coach in November 1999, Cooper—who went on to become 2000's Coach of the Year—has led the team ever since.

2: C. Nancy Lieberman (2 points)

Nancy Lieberman became the first female to play in a men's basketball league when she signed with the United States Basketball League's Springfield Flame in 1986. Lieberman, a prolific player who frequently represented the United States in international competitions, was the youngest female basketball player—at eighteen—to win an Olympic medal (silver, 1976, Montréal Games), toured with the Harlem Globetrotters in 1987–88, was a three-time Kodak All-American, played one season with the Phoenix Mercury in 1997, and was among the 1999 inaugural class of inductees to the Women's Basketball Hall of Fame.

Ann Meyers-Drysdale and Carol Blazejowski were both also honored for their contributions to the game in the Women's Basketball Hall of Fame 1999 class of inductees.

Meyers-Drysdale, the first-ever four-time Kodak All-American, was the first woman to receive a full athletic scholarship to the University of California at Los Angeles, won Olympic silver at the 1976 games in Montreal, and to this day remains the first—and only—woman ever signed to an NBA contract—as a free agent with the Indian Pacers in 1979.

Blazejowski, a three-time Kodak All-American who earned a gold medal at the World Championships and a silver at the Pan American Games in 1979, and played for the New Jersey Gems of the Women's Basketball League, still holds the women's collegiate career scoring average of 31.7 points per game.

3: C. Lisa Leslie (2 points)

A three-time Olympic gold medalist, two-time WNBA Champion, and three-time WNBA Most Valuable Player, Leslie became the first WNBA player to score five thousand career points in the WNBA in a June 25, 2006, matchup against the San Antonio Silver Stars, where she also scored a career-high forty-one game points.

Detroit Shock guard Katie Smith, who played two seasons in the American Basketball League before joining the WNBA ranks, reached the five thousand-point milestone during her time with the Minnesota Lynx against the Detroit Shock on July 13, 2005, becoming the first women's basketball player to reach the milestone as a professional.

4: D. All of the above (3 points)

Nine-year Houston Comets roster veteran guard Janeth Arcain (who retired after the 2005 season) and Seattle Storm guard Iziane Castro Marques both hail from Brazil, Hungary's Dalma Ivanyi lent her talent as a guard to the San Antonio Silver Stars and the Phoenix Mercury over the course of five WNBA seasons, and Lithuanian forward Jurgita Streimikyte spent time with the Indiana Fever.

Other countries that have seen their nationals play in the WNBA include Belgium, Canada, France, Italy, Jamaica, Nigeria, Portugal, and Russia. Foreign nationals have added depth and immeasurable talent to WNBA rosters, with some like Australia's Lauren Jackson and Tully Bevilaqua, Poland's Margo Dydek, Portugal's Ticha Penichiero, and Russia's Svetlana Abrosimova going on to be some of the WNBA's most admired and popular players.

5: A. Cheryl Ford (2 points)

Ford joined the Detroit Shock ahead of their victorious 2003 WNBA Championship-winning season. Ford averaged 10.8 points and 10.4 rebounds per game that year and was named Rookie of the Year. Since beginning her WNBA career, Ford ranks in the top five for all-time rebounds per game (averaging 10.4) and remains the only WNBA player to have won both the Championship and the Rookie of the Year award in the same year.

Fellow Rookies of the Year Betty Lennox (2000), Diana Taurasi (2004), and Seimone Augustus (2006) are all in the midst of extremely successful WNBA careers, all ranking within the top thirty all-time leaders for points per game as of the 2007 season.

6: A. Lisa Leslie and C. Sheryl Swoopes (3 points)

Both Leslie and Swoopes were members of the USA women's basketball teams to win gold medals in Atlanta (1996), Sydney (2000), and Athens (2004). Katie Smith has been on two of the gold medal-winning teams in 2000 and 2004, though she was unable to play in the 2004 medal round because of torn cartilage in her knee. Swoopes will get a shot at four in a row, Smith at the hat trick, and Augustus will take her first shot at Olympic glory at the 2008 games in Beijing, China.

7: A. Detroit Shock and B. Seattle Storm (3 points)

Though both have gone on to win WNBA Championships and inspire legions of devoted fans, neither the Detroit Shock nor the Seattle Storm were original WNBA teams. Detroit played its first season in 1998 as part of the league's first expansion efforts and Seattle joined league play in the 2000 season.

The Charlotte Sting and Houston Comets—alongside the Cleveland Rockers, Los Angeles Sparks, New York Liberty, Phoenix Mercury, Sacramento Monarchs, and Utah Starzz—were in the inaugural class of eight teams that launched WNBA play. In January 2007 the Charlotte Sting would follow the Cleveland Rockers (1997–2003) and become the second original team to fold.

8: B. Teresa Weatherspoon (2 points)

A fan vote to mark the WNBA's ten-year anniversary in 2006 for the WNBA's Greatest Moment crowned Teresa Weatherspoon's miraculous half-court, buzzer-beating basket to take the New York Liberty to victory in the second game of the 1999 finals against the Houston Comets as the WNBA's supreme moment in time. The legendary shot won out over Los Angeles Sparks' Lisa Leslie getting the first dunk in WNBA history against the Miami Sol in July 2002, and Sacramento Monarch Edna Campbell's inspiring return to the court in August 2002 after battling breast cancer.

9: B. Six (2 points)

Since the WNBA's inaugural All-Star Game in 1999, the Western Conference has won every year except 2006 and 2007. There was no All-Star Game in 2004 to allow players to participate in the Olympics.

10: D. All of the above (2 points)

Imposing seven-foot, two-inch-tall center Malgorzata "Margo" Dydek traveled from Poland to attend a WNBA predraft camp in May 1998, before the Utah Starzz selected the Warsaw native as the 1998 number-one draft pick. Dydek played with the team as it moved from Salt Lake City to San Antonio (now the Silver Stars) before heading off to play with the Connecticut Sun.

Belgian Ann Wauters was selected as the number-one draft pick in 2000 by the now-defunct Cleveland Rockers. The center moved on to play with the New York Liberty in 2004 as the result of a dispersal draft.

11: A. Lynette Woodard (2 points)

Kansas native Lynette Woodard joined the Harlem Globetrotters in 1985 as the first woman ever to play for the world renowned team. Woodard, a two-time Olympian and 1984 gold medal winner, played two seasons with the Globetrotters and was honored in 1996 with a place on the team's "Legends" ring alongside globetrotting stars Wilt "The Stilt" Chamberlain and Fred "Curly" Neal. Woodard subsequently played a season each with the Cleveland Rockers and Detroit Shock before retiring from the game.

Joyce "The Juice" Walker was the second woman to join the Harlem

Globetrotters, just a few weeks after Woodard. The two-time Kodak All-American (1983, 1984) guard out of Louisiana State University is an inductee into the Louisiana Hall of Fame who returned to her roots as the head coach at her old school, Garfield High in Seattle.

Nancy Lieberman did play alongside the Globetrotters in a 1987–88 world tour when she was playing with the United States Basketball League men's team, the Washington Generals.

Margaret Wade was a collegiate player who went on to become one of women's basketball's legendary coaches, compiling a 453–89 record at the high school level before going on to resurrect the basketball team at her old alma mater, Delta State, in 1973 at the age of sixty. Wade retired in 1979 with a 157–23 collegiate coaching record. The annual Wade Trophy is named in her honor.

12: D. Sheryl Swoopes (2 points)

Houston Comet star forward Sheryl Swoopes posted the WNBA's first-ever triple-double on July 27, 1999 in an 85–46 Comets win over the Detroit Shock, ending the game with fifteen points, fourteen rebounds, and ten assists.

Polish powerhouse center Margo Dydek became the second WNBA player to record a triple-double in an 82–70 Utah Starzz win over the Orlando Miracle on June 7, 2001. Dydek posted twelve points, eleven rebounds, and ten blocks in the game.

Sparks' center Lisa Leslie shot her way onto becoming the third woman to achieve the feat with twenty-nine points, fifteen rebounds, and ten blocks on September 10, 2004, in the Sparks' 81–63 win over the Detroit Shock.

Deanna Nolan became the fourth WNBA player to reach the feat, scoring eleven points, ten rebounds, and eleven assists in the Detroit Shock's 78–67 win over the Connecticut Sun on May 21, 2005.

13: A. 1892 (2 points)

One year after Dr. James Naismith invented the men's game of basketball, Senda Berenson adapted the rules for women's play and introduced the game to her players at Smith College.

Stanford University and the University of California at Berkeley played the first intercollegiate game in 1986. Three years later, the first rules committee was established, and in 1901 Berenson served as editor for the first official publication of the Spalding Athletic Library Basketball for Women rule book.

14: C. Ruthie Bolton and **D.** Rebecca Lobo (3 points)

Both Ruthie Bolton and Rebecca Lobo were among the first groups of players to sign on to play with the WNBA—Bolton spending her WNBA years with the Sacramento Monarchs and Rebecca Lobo playing with the New York Liberty for five years before moving on to Houston and later Connecticut.

Cynthia Cooper, Sheryl Swoopes, and Tina Thompson made up the Houston Comets triple-threat offense that led the team to an unrivaled four back-to-back WNBA Championship wins.

15: B. Lindsey Harding (2 points)

Lindsey Harding played her first WNBA season with the Minnesota Lynx after being selected 2007's number-one draft pick—more than a month after the USA 2007–08 Women's Senior National Team selections were announced.

Tamika Catchings, Alana Beard, and Cappie Pondexter join a strategic mix of veteran and up-and-coming players in the USA women's basketball's attempt to win a fourth straight Olympic gold. Other Olympic-bound WNBA and college players include Sheryl Swoopes, Katie Smith, Seimone Augustus, Sue Bird, Swin Cash, Jessica Davenport, Taj McWilliams-Franklin, Sylvia Fowles, Courtney Paris, Diana Taurasi, and Tina Thompson.

16: None. Trick question (3 points)

The WNBA did not name a Rookie of the Year for the 1997 season. Tracy Reid was the WNBA's first-ever Rookie of the Year following the 1998 season. Chamique Holdsclaw and Betty Lennox won the award in 1999 and 2000 respectively.

17: B. Take-n-run (2 points)

The full-court press is a defensive tactic wherein players guard their opponents closely for the entire length of the court as they attempt to score. An outlet pass is thrown by a player after picking off a rebound, usually to half court, while a give-and-go is a fundamental basketball play in which a player passes the ball and then cuts to the basket to receive a return pass in an attempt to score.

18: A. Kym Hampton (2 points)

The New York Liberty's Kim Hampton won the WNBA's first-ever tip-off against the Los Angeles Sparks Lisa Leslie on June 21, 1997. The Liberty would go on to win the game 67–57.

Lisa Leslie, Mwadi Mabika, and Vickie Johnson, plus Sheryl Swoopes and Wendy Palmer-David, were among a handful of players from the inaugural season still on rosters at the tenth-anniversary mark.

19: D. Margo Dydek (2 points)

Poland's Malgorzata "Margo" Dydek became the first-ever international player drafted by a WNBA team, when the Utah Starzz drafted the center following her attendance at a predraft WNBA camp in May 1998.

Canada's Tammy Sutton-Brown joined the Charlotte Sting's starting lineup in the center's 2001 rookie year and remained with the team until it folded in January 2007 before moving on to play with the Indiana Fever. Australian guard Tully Bevilaqua has played across the WNBA, building on three years with the Portland Fire to become a 2004 WNBA Champion during her two seasons with the Seattle Storm, before moving to the Indiana Fever roster in 2005. Her fellow Australian Lauren Jackson has played her WNBA career with the Seattle Storm, emerging as one of the team's most prolific scorers, and was also a member of the 2004 WNBA Championship-winning team.

20: B. 1980 (2 points)

The USA Women's Senior National Team medaled in every Olympic Games in the three decades since the sport was introduced at the 1976 Montreal games, where the USA team won a silver medal. The only time the American women did not medal was 1980, when the United States boycotted the Moscow games. Overall the women's teams amassed five gold, one silver, and one bronze in their seven Olympic appearances through the 2004 games.

21: C. Point guard (2 points)

A point guard handles the ball more than any other player on the team, and is a prodigious ball handler and passer with a key eye for reading defensive positioning and matchups. The center, who is usually the tallest player on the team, is—among other things—an under-the-basket defender with uncommon skill in rebounds and shot blocking. The power forward is usualy a team's chief rebounder on both ends of the court. A shooting guard is usually one of the team's highest scoring players, with fierce, long-range shooting capabilities.

22: B. Olympic medal winner (2 points)

The WNBA All-Decade Team (ten players, one each for every year) was chosen to celebrate the league's ten-year anniversary by fans, current players, coaches, and media members from a pool of thirty nominees. Choices were based on a variety of factors including sportsmanship, on-the-court ability, and community service. All ten of the following women are Olympic medal winners: Sue Bird, Tamika Catchings, Cynthia Cooper, Yolanda Griffith, Lauren Jackson, Lisa Leslie, Katie Smith, Dawn Staley, Tina Thompson, and Sheryl Swoopes.

23: D. Fast break (2 points)

A fast break is an offensive maneuver wherein the team moves quickly across the court in the hopes of scoring before the other team has a chance to set its defense. A half-court press is a defensive tactic in which the defending team players pick up and guard their opponents closely at the half-court line. Man-to-man coverage will see a defensive player shadow an assigned offensive player wherever she moves on the court. Defensive players will double-team the player with the ball in a "trap" designed to force a turnover or jump ball.

24: C. Japan (2 points)

Teams representing six countries—Bulgaria, Canada, Czechoslovakia, Japan, the United States, and the USSR—competed the first year women's basketball was introduced as an Olympic sport in 1976. The Soviet Union took home the first-ever Olympic gold medal. The United States took silver and Bulgaria, the bronze.

25: D. All of the above (2 points)

The American Heart Association, Nothing But Nets, and the March of Dimes are among the dozens of organizations, associations, and institutions with which the WNBA partners in its efforts to reach out to communities across the country and make a difference in young peoples' lives.

SCORING

0-15 points: FOUL! Did you even read the book?!?!

16-25 points: BENCHED! Go back to page one and reread!

26-35 points: You know your stuff, but there's still plenty to learn.

36-45 points: Champion-level knowledge; you are ready for the big game!

46 points or higher: Call the networks, 'cause they need to hire you!

Glossary

This dictionary of basketball terms was created with the generous help of WNBA legend Kym Hampton.

and-one: slang term for when an offensive player is fouled in the process of making a basket; refers to the free throw awarded as a result of the foul

assist: a pass that leads directly to the scoring of points

baby hook: a hook shot that is taken from very close to the basket, in which the ball is simply flicked over the rim

backboard: structure to which the basket is attached

backcourt: (1) a team's defensive half of the court; (2) a team's guards

ball fake: a core offensive basketball skill in which a player fakes a pass or shot to lure a defender off balance and open up a passing, shooting, or driving lane

bank shot: a shot where the ball bounces (or banks) off the backboard before dropping into the basket.

blocked shot: a defensive move to prevent an offensive player's shot from reaching the basket

box out: an offensive or defensive move to position oneself in front of a player for optimal rebounding position

brick: a shot on basket that hits the rim or backboard and careens wildly away from the basket

bricklayer: a player who shoots a high percentage of bricks

charging: an offensive violation when a player runs into an immobile opponent

charity stripe: Slang for the free throw line (see foul/free throw line for more)

chest pass: a two-handed pass thrown from one player's chest directly to the chest area of a receiving player

coast-to-coast: from one end of the court to the other

controlling the boards: obtaining the majority of rebounds

double-double: scoring in double digits in two of the main statistical categories of points, rebounds, assists, steals, and blocks

double team: a defensive approach that involves two players guarding one player from the opposing team

drive: a fast move straight at the basket in an attempt to score

dunk: occurs when a player close to the basket jumps and slams the ball down through the basket (a.k.a. "slam dunk")

fast break: a play in which a team gains possession and moves quickly toward the opposing basket in the hopes of taking a shot before the other team can set its defense

field goal: any basket, other than a free throw, worth two or three points depending on the distance from the basket. Baskets made from beyond the twenty-foot, three-point line are worth three points.

finger roll: a layup shot where the ball originates in the flat palm of a player's hand, and as the player raises the ball overhead it is rolled off the fingers into the basket

foul: a punishable violation usually involving illegal contact with a player from the opposing team

foul/free throw line: a line, fifteen feet from each basket, from where players attempt shots awarded as a result of fouls

free throw: a shot taken by a player from behind the foul line after a foul or violation has occurred. Each successful free throw is worth one point.

front court: (1) a team's offensive half of the court; (2) a team's center and forwards

full-court press: A defensive tactic in which a team's players guard their opponents closely for the length of the court in an attempt to rush the opposing team, steal the ball, or pressure the opposing team into making a mistake

give-and-go: a basic skill in which one player passes the ball to a teammate, then cuts toward the basket to receive a pass and take a shot

half-court press: A defensive tactic in which the defending team's players begin to guard their opponents closely after they cross the mid-court line in an attempt to force a turnover, make a steal, or pressure the opposing team into making a mistake

high-percentage shot: a shot that statistically is likely to go into the basket for a score

high post: the area of the court near the free-throw line

jump ball: the play that starts a game, when a referee tosses the ball in the air between two players from opposing teams who each try to tip the ball to a teammate; also used to break the stalemate when two opposing players gain possession of the ball at the same time

jump shot: a shot usually taken from five feet or more from the basket, usually involving a player's feet leaving the floor

layup: a shot taken from a position close to the basket

low post: area of the court near the basket

man-to-man: a defensive tactic in which every defensive player is assigned a specific offensive player to guard wherever they move on the court

outlet pass: a pass thrown after recovering possession of the ball to initiate an offensive charge to the opposing basket

the paint: the painted area of the court, present on both ends from the baseline to the free-throw line

rebound: when a player gains possession of the ball after a shot at the basket

rim out: occurs after a shot is taken, where the ball rolls around the rim but bounces out of the basket at the last second

run: when one team is able to score a series of field goals rapidly without allowing the opposing team to answer with an equitable amount of its own point scoring

shot clock: the clock that tracks the amount of time a team has to attempt a score and hit the rim after taking possession of the ball or lose offensive possession to the other team

steal: when a player takes the ball away from the opposing team, usually by picking off a pass or taking it off the dribble

technical foul: a foul that does not necessarily involve direct bodily contact; often assessed for unsportsmanlike conduct by players or members of the coaching staff. Each "technical" results in a free throw, a change in ball possession, and an automatic fine for players

transition: when a team switches from offense to defense, or vice versa, as possession of the ball changes

traveling: a violation involving illegal foot movement by the offensive player in possession of the ball

triple-double: scoring in double digits in three of the main statistical categories of points, rebounds, assists, steals, and blocks

weak side: the side of the court away from the ball

zone: a defensive tactic in which defensive players are assigned an area on the court to defend rather than a specific offensive player

Acknowledgments

From the moment I began writing this book, I discovered that this journey could not have progressed without the help and support of many generous souls.

Special thanks must be given to my husband, Asad, who "lost" his wife to the back study for the better part of eight months and had to repeatedly climb through the mountain-esque pile of research notes to see if I wanted dinner. And to my in-laws, Mr. and Mrs. Malik Riaz, who spent their two-month vacation taking care of the house, the cooking, and all the other work from which they were supposed to be taking a break.

Heartfelt thanks to those inside the basketball world who took the time, and had the patience, to guide a newbie through some of the nuances of this incredible league: Tauja and Tamika Catchings, Betty Lennox, Leslie Cole, Kym Hampton, Rebecca Lobo, Jayda Evans, Helen Wheelock, Melissa Sterry, Lisa Pelofsky, Stephen Burt, Steve Rice, Clay Kallam, David Seigel, Kim Bittinger at the Women's Basketball Hall of Fame in Knoxville, Tennessee, and many, many others.

The high points are thanks to their help; the mistakes, all mine!

And a huge shout-out to the ladies and gentlemen at Alyson Books, who dedicated their time and efforts into making this book a reality.